THE TRUTH ABOUT

ADHD

GENUINE HOPE AND BIBLICAL ANSWERS

By

Dr. Daniel R. Berger II

The Truth about ADHD: Genuine Hope and Biblical Answers
Library of Congress Control Number: 2015900157
Trade Paperback ISBN: 978-0-9864114-0-3

Published by Alethia International Publications
        Taylors, SC - USA

drberger.dr@gmail.com

Printed in the United States of America.

To

my loving father and mother

"Train up [dedicate] a child in the way he should go;

even when he is old he will not depart from it."

Proverbs 22:6

ACKNOWLEDGEMENTS

I first want to thank my Lord Jesus Christ, whose grace is both the reason for writing this book and the reason my own mindsets, emotions, and behaviors are changing to reflect His character. Additionally, God allowed me the privilege of administrating and pastoring in numerous ministries that forced me to search and study-out practical answers and hope for our human needs. Specifically, I want to thank Pastor Marc Mortensen at First Baptist Church of Westwood Lakes Miami for allowing me the opportunity to pastor alongside of him, counsel under his leadership, and for his continued friendship.

I also want to thank my wife, Oriana, for her love, patience, support, and prayer for this project, our home, and ministries. It will never be known on this side of eternity the amount of sacrifices she has made to support me. Furthermore, I want to thank my parents and grandparents for their own teaching of God's wisdom that modelled true love for God and the pursuit of His wisdom above all other passions.

Likewise, my close friends and teachers throughout my life have been an encouragement, a sounding board, and a group of solid counselors throughout the last decade of research and writing. I am blessed to have such godly and faithful friends who interceded for me and patiently waited for the final product.

I wish to also thank my editor, Laurie Buck, who diligently and patiently edited this book. I cannot thank her enough for her hard work, encouragement, and contributions.

TABLE OF CONTENTS

ABBREVIATIONS

AAP	American Academy of Pediatrics
APA	American Psychological Association
ADD	Attention Deficit Disorder
ADHD	Attention Deficit Hyperactivity Disorder
ADHD-I	Attention Deficit Hyperactivity Disorder – Inattentive type
ADHD-HI	Attention Deficit Hyperactivity Disorder – Hyperactivity-Impulsivity type
ADHD-C	Attention Deficit Hyperactivity Disorder – Combined type
DSM	*The Diagnostic and Statistical Manual of Mental Disorders IV*-TR
ESV	English Standard Version
KJV	King James Version
NAS	New American Standard
NIMH	National Institute of Mental Health
NoSC	*ADHD and the Nature of Self-Control*
ODD	Oppositional-Defiant Disorder
TCoA	*Taking Control of ADHD*

INTRODUCTION

Several years ago I was, like many parents, teachers, and counselors, searching for answers to help children diagnosed with Attention Deficit Hyperactivity Disorder (ADHD). The more I read and the more I interviewed leading psychiatrists, psychologists, so-called experts, and pediatricians, the more I realized that they too were searching for reliable answers to the issues surrounding what is commonly referred to as ADHD or ADD.[1] As a Christian, I am convinced that the Bible is sufficient to meet our needs for life and godliness, but it seemed to me for some time that ADHD was outside the scope of the Scripture's ability to help and answer pressing questions. Ironically, while reading a secular psychology textbook, I discovered a striking observation by psychotherapy researcher Jerome Frank,[2] which began to redirect my thinking about ADHD back to the Scriptures: "Psychotherapy may be the only treatment that creates the illness it treats."[3] Frank's observation suggesting that

---

[1] Attention Deficit Disorder (ADD) is an older label used to describe what is commonly referred to as ADHD today. Many professionals still use ADD over ADHD in their literature and counseling.

[2] "Obituary: Jerome Frank, 95, Noted Psychotherapy Researcher," *Johns Hopkins Gazette* 34, no. 30 (April 18, 2005); available from www.jhu.edu/gazette/2005/18apr05/18frank.html; Internet.

[3] Mark Bubble, Barry Duncan, and Scott Miller, *The Heart and Soul of Change: What Works in Therapy* (Washington, D.C.: American Psychological Association, 1999), 2.

psychotherapy created disorders such as ADHD, however, was only partially correct: psychotherapy had created the label of ADHD and described the label as a disease defined and treated by the medical model,[4] but psychotherapy did not create the human behaviors and heart conditions that constitute the descriptive label. These behaviors are found in every culture throughout history.

When focused on the ADHD label, I had overlooked that the behaviors, the heart and life conditions, and the biblical solutions all existed prior to the use of the current label. Simply stated, though the secular label (currently ADHD) that describes a child's behaviors is relatively new, in truth, nothing is new under the sun (Eccl 1:9-10).[5]

Definition of Terms

For the sake of clarity, it is helpful first to define some terms that will be used in this book. One such term is *biblical parental discipline*. This term is used to reflect the parents' efforts, faith, and lifestyle that direct their children toward regeneration and intimacy with God. The biblical idea of discipline differs greatly from the secular usage and philosophy. In fact, discipline in Scripture is centered on God's wisdom and the heart rather than on behavioral changes and is focused on a clear and well-established goal. Biblical parental discipline or discipleship, then, should be understood as the parents' obedience to God's Word and love for their children that drive them to educate their children in the

---

[4] Russell A. Barkley, *ADHD and the Nature of Self-Control* (New York: Guilford, 2005), 31-32. Hereafter referred to as *NoSC*.

[5] The *ESV* will be used throughout this book unless otherwise noted.

biblical way.[6] Therefore the biblical idea of discipline is not punishment, but rather guidance from point A to point B: a clear goal or priority has been established by the authority, and all efforts and actions are in accordance with accomplishing these goals. If parents desire their children to be wise disciples of Christ, they must biblically discipline their children. Biblical discipline should not be misunderstood or equated with secularists' view of discipline that focuses not on salvation or sanctification but rather on behavior modification. Biblical discipline is concerned with the child's heart, which, when being regenerated and renewed by the work of the Holy Spirit, will produce corresponding behaviors that please God.

Along with biblical parental discipline, the scriptural concept of a fool, especially from Proverbs, is important to understand. All children begin life in a foolish state. Proverbs pronounces foolishness to be bound in each child's heart (22:15; point A) and establishes wisdom as the necessary direction/goal that parents must lead their children toward (29:15; point B). This process or dedication from point A or B (22:6) is referred to in Scripture as discipline. Since the term *fool* can be confusing and upsetting if not properly understood, and since it is an integral part of both Proverbs and this book, detailed attention to defining a fool is provided as an appendix. Writer William McKane effectively explains that biblical parental discipline is both a philosophy of education and

---

[6] "Godly wisdom is not lightly picked up (12; cf. verse 23), nor lightly imparted (13, 14): the same word *mûsār* (discipline, training) is used in 12a as in 13a. The brisk 13b can be taken in two ways, and 14 underlines the second of them: the child will not only survive it, he will survive *because* of it" (Derek Kidner, *Proverbs: An Introduction and Commentary*, vol. 17, Tyndale Old Testament Commentaries (Downers Grove, IL: InterVarsity Press, 1964), 144).

the parents' God-given means to address the child's naturally foolish heart and point him toward being Christ's disciple:

> There is more to education than making manifest what is already there or hastening the maturity of the seed which already contains all the possibilities of growth and nothing that would hinder it. The educator's task is both to tear down and to build up; he has to eradicate as well as to implant. There are elements of chaos in the mind of the youth and order has to be restored; *his innate tendency is towards folly rather than wisdom, and only the sebet musar will put a distance between him and folly.* This is not just a reference to corporal punishment, though it includes this. **It is an indication of a theory of education which comes down strongly on the side of discipline,** but the most important application of this is not corporal punishment. It is rather the emphasis on the intellectual authority of the teacher and *the duty of unbroken attentiveness* and unquestioning acceptance which is laid upon the pupil [emphasis added].[7]

Additionally, *comorbid* is a medical term used to refer to two or more diseases that coexist in the body independently of any other medical disorder.[8] In a similar way, the term is used in psychology to refer to the presence of two or more disorders that coexist. This book uses the term as secularists do in discussion of *Oppositional-Defiant Disorder* (ODD), which is often referred to as a comorbid condition of ADHD. Secularists diagnose children as having ODD in approximately half of all children they diagnose as having ADHD.[9]

---

[7] William McKane, *Proverbs: A New Approach* (Philadelphia: Westminster, 1970), 564-65.

[8] "Comorbidity can be simply defined as two or more diseases occurring in the same individual" (Steven R. Pliszka, *Treating ADHD and Comorbid Disorders: Psychosocial and Psychopharmacological Interventions* [New York: Guilford, 2009], 2). See also "Comorbidity"; available from http://www.merriam-webster.com/dictionary/ comorbid; Internet.

[9] American Psychiatric Association, *Diagnostic and Statistical Manual of Mental Disorders: DSM-IV-TR* (Washington, D.C.: American Psychiatric Association, 2000), 88. Hereafter referred to as *DSM*.

CHAPTER 1 – UNDERSTANDING THE ADHD LABEL

Attention Deficit Hyperactivity Disorder (ADHD) is a controversial, alleged disorder[1] affecting as many as 11 percent[2] of U.S. children and as high as 18 percent in some schools.[3] Though these figures are disputable,[4] hundreds of families and educators experience frustration over the diagnoses of ADHD and desire reliable answers.[5] So what is ADHD?

---

[1] Leigh Pretnar Cousins, "Might Schools Be Teaching ADHD?"; available from http://psychcentral.com/lib/2010/might-schools-be-teaching-adhd/; Internet.

[2] According to the Centers for Disease Control and Prevention, diagnoses of ADHD in the last decade have risen to include 11 percent ("Key Findings: Trends in the Parent-Report of Health Care Provider-Diagnosis and Medication Treatment for ADHD: United States, 2003-2011"; available from http://www.cdc.gov/ncbddd /adhd/features/key-findings-adhd72013.html; Internet) of all American children compared to almost 8 percent in 2003 (Maggie Fox, "Number of Young Adults on ADHD Drugs Soars"; available from http://www.nbcnews.com/health/health-news/number-young-adults-adhd-drugs-soars-n50856; Internet; accessed 12 March 2014). The American Psychiatric Association claims only 5 percent of American children have ADHD ibid).

[3] Julian Haber, *ADHD: The Great Misdiagnosis* (New York: Taylor Trade, 2003), 1.

[4] Paul Wender claims 10 percent is more accurate. *ADHD: Attention-Deficit Hyperactivity Disorder in Children, Adolescents, and Adults* (New York: Oxford University Press, 2000), 4.

[5] Edward M. Hallowell and John J. Ratey, *Driven to Distraction: Recognizing and Coping with Attention Deficit Disorder from Childhood through Adulthood* (New York: Pantheon Books, 1994), i.

The Premise of the DSM

In order to answer the afore mentioned question one must first become familiar with the ideas about ADHD presented in the *Diagnostic and Statistical Manual of Mental Disorders,*[6] hereafter referred to as the *DSM*. Secular psychology in general considers this book to be the authority on ADHD (and many other alleged disorders) and claims it contains "some of the most rigorous and most empirically derived criteria ever available in the history of clinical diagnosis."[7] Because most clinicians consider the *DSM* to be authoritative and empirically sound, it is the primary tool used to describe ADHD and to establish the diagnostic process.[8] In regards to ADHD, the *DSM* and the diagnostic system are based entirely on observations of a child's "maladaptive behaviors."[9] Secularists divide the *DSM*'s classification of ADHD into two main categories which consist of nine observable behaviors in each group: *inattention* and the combination of *hyperactivity-impulsivity*. At least six of the nine behaviors in one group or the other must be observable in a child's life over a period of at least six months. Furthermore, "there must be clear evidence of clinically significant impairment

---

[6] American Psychiatric Association, *Diagnostic and Statistical Manual of Mental Disorders: DSM-IV-TR* (Washington, D.C.: American Psychiatric Association, 2000). Currently, the American Psychiatric Association has published a fifth revision of the *DSM*. The changes to the new addition regarding ADHD were not significant, and the general premise of the ADHD label remains the same. Therefore, this book uses the *DSM-IV* in citations, since the majority of the book was written prior to the publishing of the *DSM-V*.

[7] Russell A. Barkley, *ADHD and the Nature of Self-Control* (New York: Guilford, 2005), 14. Hereafter referred to as *NoSC*.

[8] Melody Petersen, *Our Daily Meds* (New York: Sarah Crichton Books, 2008), 98. Many secularists are beginning to realize that the *DSM* is not a standard or even an authority but merely a set of manmade guidelines (Richard Saul, *ADHD Does Not Exist: The Truth about Attention Deficit and Hyperactivity Disorder* [New York: HarperCollins, 2014], 178).

[9] Wender, *ADHD*, 159.

in social, academic, or occupational functioning."[10] Symptoms must also be present in a child prior to age seven; they must be present in at least two different life environments (typically school and home); they must socially, academically, or occupationally impair the child; and they must not be mistaken for other disorders that are environmentally caused or meet similar criteria.[11] The child's behaviors also distinguish which subtype of ADHD he allegedly has: "predominantly inattention (ADHD-I), predominantly hyperactive-impulsive (ADHD-HI), and combined type (ADHD-C)."[12] A fourth subtype of ADHD also exists for children who exhibit strong ADHD tendencies without fully meeting the diagnostic requirements. Psychiatrists refer to this type of ADHD as "Not Otherwise Specified."[13]

Though society in general often equates hyperactivity to ADHD, secular therapists distinguish ADHD behavior from mere hyperactivity through their system of measurements and qualifications in the *DSM*. Familiarity with these qualifications provides invaluable understanding and lays the groundwork for the following chapters.

The Nature of the DSM and the Diagnostic Process

We began this chapter asking what is ADHD? Answering this question is neither simple nor straightforward. Secularists Hallowell and Ratey

---

[10] *DSM*, 83-85.

[11] Ibid., 90-93.

[12] *NoSC*, 14.

[13] *DSM*, 93. We will discuss this subtype further in this chapter.

8

acknowledge this difficulty as well: "We do not have one concise definition for ADD. Instead, we have to rely on descriptions of symptoms to define ADD."[14] Why would there not be a concise definition? If we asked the question, "What is cancer?" a concise definition could easily be offered. This lack of concrete definition exposes the nature of ADHD and reveals what it is truly. ADHD is a construct:

> Constructs are abstract concepts of something that is not real in the physical sense that a spoon or motorcycle or cat can be seen and touched. Constructs are shared ideas, supported by general agreement. . . . Mental illness is a construct. . . . The category itself is an invention, a creation. It may be a good and useful invention, or it may be a confusing one. DSM is a compendium of constructs. And like a large and popular mutual fund, DSM's holdings are constantly changing[15]

Simply stated, a group of like-minded people have taken a child's unwanted observable behaviors and created a label and subsequent theories in attempts to explain, deal with, and remedy them. Yet these attempts, by their own confessions, have been unsuccessful. So when we speak of ADHD, we are talking about a construct or theory of anthropology and behavior rather than an actual measurable/tangible thing. Denying the construct, however, is not in any way denying that the child has behavioral problems, which need to be addressed, it simply denies an unproven, ever-changing theory as we will observe.

In addition to understanding the premise of the DSM and the ADHD construct, counselors and parents must also comprehend the overwhelming subjectivity of both the DSM criteria and the diagnostic process. Though

---

[14] Driven to Distraction, 151.

[15] Herb Kutchins and Stuart A. Kirk, Making us Crazy: DSM: The Psychiatric Bible and the Creation of Mental Disorders (New York: Free Press, 1997), 22-25.

psychiatrists admit that "problems and critical issues still remain,"[16] they continue to claim scientific validity for the *DSM*.[17] In short, the *DSM* criteria for ADHD (and the proposed diagnostic process) are subjective descriptions of behavior rather than a scientific definition of a disease.[18]

It is important to note that ADHD symptoms are not abnormal but rather "fall within the normal range of human behavior."[19] Many doctors perceive the normalcy of ADHD criteria as indicating an alarming subjectivity in the diagnostic process.

> We are convinced if a research team were able through some Orwellian act of Congress to assess every child in America between the ages of five and twelve, and said team adhered strictly to *DSM* guidelines, they would find that close to half of all elementary-age children in America qualify for at least one of these diagnoses. . . . The *DSM* criteria, when objectively and dispassionately applied, describe so many of today's kids is alarming, if not chilling.[20]

Respected therapists also concede that ADHD behaviors are normal in American society and suggest that culture is disordered, rather than children:

> American society tends to create ADD-like symptoms in us all. We live in an ADD-ogenic culture . . . the fast pace. The sound bite. The bottom line. Short takes, quick cuts. The TV remote-control clicker. High stimulation. Restlessness. Violence. Anxiety. Ingenuity. . . . It is important to keep this in mind or you may start thinking that

---

[16] *NoSC*, 14.

[17] Russell A. Barkley, Kevin R. Murphy, and Mariellen Fischer, *ADHD in Adults: What the Science Says* (New York: Guilford, 2008), 38-39.

[18] Carol Tavris, *Psychobabble and Biobunk: Using Psychological Science to Think Critically about Popular Psychology* (Upper Saddle, N.J.: Prentice Hall, 2001), 102.

[19] Katherine Ellison, "Brain Scans Link ADHD to Biological Flaw Tied to Motivation"; available from http://www.washingtonpost.com/wpdyn/content/article/2009/09/21/AR2009092103100.html; Internet.

[20] Rosemond, John, and Bose Ravenel, *The Diseasing of America's Children: Exposing the ADHD Fiasco and Empowering Parents to Take Back Control* (Nashville: Thomas Nelson, 2008), 105-07.

everybody you know has ADD. The disorder is culturally syntonic — that is to say, it fits right in.[21]

One aim of the *DSM* is to distinguish abnormal social behavior from normal. The *DSM* attempts to distinguish ADHD from normalcy by the frequency of behavioral occurrences and the degree to which these behaviors impair the child's life. Wender stresses that the frequency of behavior determines abnormality: "Let me emphasize that the characteristics listed are not abnormal in themselves; they are only abnormal when they are excessive." But who decides what is excessive? Wender also believes that "the intensity, the persistence, and the patterning of these symptoms"[22] determine whether a child has ADHD. The *DSM* lists two seemingly objective qualifications to determine behavioral frequency: symptoms must be present for at least six months and some symptoms must be present prior to the age of seven.[23] Some therapists dismiss the latter qualification as nebulous since almost all children exhibit hyperactivity and impulsivity prior to age seven.[24] The other seemingly objective qualification is the persistence of six of the nine criteria for at least six months. Even in this assessment, however, clinicians must subjectively determine what qualifies as persistent.

The *DSM* verbiage further ensures that diagnoses be subjective by qualifying each criterion with the word *often*. This qualification undermines validity as "dependence on the word 'often' to define 'symptoms' of ADHD

---

[21] Hallowell and Ratey, *Driven to Distraction*, 191.

[22] Wender, *ADHD*, 9.

[23] *DSM*, 92-93. The *DSM-V* has changed that age to 12.

[24] Rosemond and Ravenel, 107.

reduces the disorder to one of personal taste, having nothing to do with any scientific, medical, or objective criteria."[25] Reliable standards of measurement in the diagnostic process cannot exist since opinions often vacillate and conflict, compromising the claim that the ADHD construct is a scientific fact.[26]

Not only are the individual criteria written subjectively, but so also are the main classifications of behavior. For example, the therapist must determine when a child has persistent inattention, hyperactivity, or impulsivity to a degree that is maladaptive and inconsistent with developmental level.[27] This phraseology assumes the existence of a normative measurement of age-appropriate behavior. Since this standard is non-existent, the therapist must subjectively compare how a child compares to others his age. The variance in developmental rates of children adds to the diagnostic complexity and renders validity and objectivity impossible.[28]

Further undermining the validity of the ADHD construct as a physiological disorder is the proposed theory that ADHD is a disorder only when it impairs a child's life.[29] Renowned secular authors on ADHD Hallowell and Ratey insist that "for many people, ADD is not a disorder but a trait, a way

---

[25] Stephen Flora, *Taking America off Drugs: Why Behavioral Therapy is More Effective for Treating ADHD, OCD, Depression, and Other Psychological Problems* (New York: State University of New York Press, 2007), 77.

[26] Rosemond and Ravenel, 17.

[27] *DSM*, 85.

[28] Bruce Pennington, *Diagnosing Learning Disorders: A Neuropsychological Framework*, 2nd ed. (New York: Guilford, 2009), 4.

[29] Edward M. Hallowell and John J. Ratey, *Delivered from Distraction: Getting the Most out of Life with Attention Deficit Disorder* (New York: Ballantine Books, 2005), 4.

of being in the world."[30] In their view, ADHD is a "positive character quality" that provides many gifts and talents until behavior becomes maladaptive.[31] Their logic suggests that ADHD is a matter of character when it is beneficial and a disease when it is maladaptive. Clinicians are left to determine when behavior is dysfunctional by relying solely on their own perception. Consequently, since subjective observation and authoritative testimony are the substance of every diagnosis, some children and adults manipulate evaluations in order to obtain prescription stimulants.[32]

However, clinicians are not alone in making subjective evaluations of children: the current diagnostic system requires the parents,[33] teachers[34] and other authorities to evaluate, compare, and identify children through measurement systems such as the "Behavioral Rating Scales" (BRS). Psychotherapy bases this rating system on a standardized form, yet the BRS relies on the subjective opinions and observations of the administrator.[35] Barkley admits that these rating scales are circular in reasoning, though he argues that external measurements eliminate circularity.[36]

---

[30] Ibid.

[31] Ibid.

[32] "Risky Ritalin Abuse during College Exam Week"; available from http://ihealthbulletin.com/archive/2007/05/14/risky-ritalin-abuse-during-college-exam-week/; Internet.

[33] Vincent J. Monastra, *Parenting Children with ADHD: 10 Lessons that Medicine Cannot Teach* (Washington, D.C.: American Psychological Association, 2005), 17.

[34] Rosemond and Ravenel, 69.

[35] Pennington, 166.

[36] *NoSC*, 66.

Another factor in the diagnostic process that yields disagreement among professionals is a child's level of maturity, as children must be compared to other children of the same age:

> Several earlier studies have also found a higher incidence of ADHD among the youngest children in classrooms, suggesting that less mature children may be inappropriately labeled and treated for ADHD. "It certainly appears that in some cases lack of maturity is being misinterpreted as ADHD, and it raises alarms about over-diagnosis," says researcher Richard L. Morrow of the University of British Columbia.[37]

Though Wender, believes ADHD is under-diagnosed, he concedes that immaturity describes ADHD well: "Immaturity is neither a very scientific nor a very specific word, but it often does accurately describe the behavior of ADHD children."[38] The reality of immaturity as a probable cause of maladaptive behavior has led to the creation of new unofficial labels to describe misdiagnoses such as "faux-ADHD"[39] and "pseudo–ADHD."[40] These labels provide therapists he opportunity to dismiss children from the ADHD diagnosis, though other therapists perceive them as meeting the *DSM* requirements. Many therapists

---

[37] Salynn Boyles, "Immaturity Mistaken for ADHD?: Youngest Kids in the Classroom More Likely to Be Diagnosed"; available from http://children .webmd.com/news/20120305/is-immaturity-being-mistaken-adhd?ecd=wnl_prg_031112; Internet.

[38] Wender, *ADHD*, 28.

[39] Robert Pressman and Steve Imber, "Relationship of Children's Daytime Behavior Problems with Bedtime Routines/Practices: A Family Context and the Consideration of Faux-ADHD"; available from http://www.pedipsyc.com/abstract_FauxADHD.php; Internet; accessed 21 September 2011; Daniel DeNoon, "Kids' Poor Bedtime Habits May Bring ADHD Misdiagnosis"; available from http://www.webmd.com/add-adhd/news/20110919/kids-poor-bedtime-habits-may-bring-adhd-misdiagnosis; Internet.

[40] Edward Hallowell, "Dr. Hallowell's Response to NY Times Piece 'Ritalin Gone Wrong'"; available from http://www.drhallowell.com/blog/dr-hallowells-response-to-ny-mes-piece-ritalin-gone-wrong/; Internet.

reason that since environmental influences, such as poor diets or lack of sleep,[41] have caused these behaviors and not theoretical causes (genetics, chemical imbalances, and neurological abnormalities), the child cannot have ADHD.
.

The *DSM* further reveals or rather opens the door for more subjectivity in the final criterion for ADHD, which states that therapists should evaluate thoroughly whether the observed behaviors might be attributable to another disorder or influence. Clinicians must subjectively assess whether a child's behaviors are characteristic of ADHD or whether they have another cause. Of this qualification Monastra writes, "In my opinion, the final criterion for ADHD is often ignored or minimized by health care professionals. It requires that the doctor diagnosing ADHD ensure that the symptoms of inattention, impulsivity, or hyperactivity are not caused by another mental or physical disorder."[42] Monastra also states that in conducting over 10,000 patient evaluations, rarely did he find that other physicians previously tested ADHD patients for sleep apnea, allergies, thyroid disorders, or other physical influences.[43]

Subjectivity in the diagnostic process likewise results from the absence of reliable tests to measure the presence of ADHD. The *DSM* states, "There are no laboratory tests, neurological assessments, or attentional assessments that have been established as diagnostic in the clinical assessment of Attention-

---

[41] Russell A. Barkley, *Taking Charge of ADHD: A Complete Authoritative Guide for Parents.* rev. ed. (New York: Guilford, 2000), 75-79. Hereafter referred to as *TCoA.*

[42] Monastra, 23.

[43] Ibid.

Deficit/Hyperactivity Disorder."[44] One seemingly potential diagnostic tool is the use of brain imaging such as an MRI scanner, yet these types of scanners are currently used only in research.[45] Even if some variant in the brain is someday discovered through scans, we will not know from these studies if the abnormality is the cause or the effect of bad behavior. The absence of an objective diagnostic test results in unreliable diagnoses and reliance on therapists' perception.

> The diagnosis of ADHD is difficult, both because of the number of confounding conditions that must be excluded, and because objective tests of ADHD are less well developed than those for dyslexia or other learning disorders. So clinicians should be duly cautious in making this diagnosis. . . . Although objective tests for ADHD are not well developed, testing results can often support the diagnosis by identifying underlying cognitive deficits that are often present in ADHD.[46]

The diagnostic subjectivity leads to confusion and differing opinions on rates of ADHD in society. Since no objective test exists,[47] therapists have only subjective evaluations to apply, and disagreement on who has ADHD is prevalent.

> Diagnosing ADHD takes good clinical detective work," says child psychiatrist Ismail Sendi of Michigan's Henry Ford Health System. Sendi tested 388 Michigan children who were taking Ritalin. He found that only sixty-seven had been correctly diagnosed. "The other 82 percent should have been getting treatment for another disorder.[48]

The difficulty and probable impossibility of proper diagnosis have led many professionals to form strong opinions about the rate of ADHD diagnoses.

---

[44] *DSM*, 88-89.

[45] Thomas Insel, "Brain Scans: Not Quite Ready for Prime Time"; available from http://www.nimh.nih.gov/about/director/index-adhd.shtml; Internet.

[46] Pennington, 166.

[47] Petersen, 98.

[48] Francha Roffé Menhard, *Drugs: The Facts about Ritalin* (New York: Marshall Cavendish Benchmark, 2007), 26.

Some insist that ADHD is under-diagnosed,[49] while others argue that it is assigned to children way too often.[50] The American Academy of Pediatrics (AAP) published a clinical guideline for diagnosing ADHD in which it expresses this concern for proper diagnoses: "The *DSM* system does not specifically provide for developmental-level differences and might lead to some misdiagnoses."[51] These misdiagnoses are a product of the subjective nature of the *DSM* and the diagnostic system it espouses.

Finally, subjectivity exists in the selection of criteria for the *DSM*. When psychiatrists selected the current system of measurement, they included only eighteen behaviors. No standard of exclusion/inclusion existed for determining ADHD criteria. The *DSM III* (1987) contained different criteria for the ADHD construct than does the *DSM-IV* and *V* (1996).[52] The *DSM III* also required the existence of eight of fourteen symptomatic behaviors in a child compared to six of nine in the *DSM-IV* and *V*. In both editions, committees subjectively chose which behaviors (and the quantity) should compose the criteria for diagnosing ADHD – a benefit of creating a construct. Many therapists have observed the label's limitation in describing the spectrum of behaviors associated with the label: "Many behavioral scientists, neurologists, parents, educators, and

---

[49] Marie Hartwell-Walker, "It May Not Be ADHD"; available from http://psychcentral.com/lib/2010/it-may-not-be-adhd; Internet.

[50] Haber, 2-3.

[51] "Clinical Practice Guideline for the Diagnosis, Evaluation, and Treatment of Attention-Deficit/Hyperactivity Disorder in Children and Adolescents"; available from http://pediatrics.aappublications.org/content/early/2011/10/14/peds.2011-2654; Internet.

[52] Haber, 32.

pediatricians would like to see a name for the disorder that would better capture all of the varied problems these children have."[53] Therapists who were not on the *DSM* selection committee often see the *DSM* qualifications as inadequately describing the true nature of ADHD children.[54] Such disagreement reveals a problem of subjectivity with the *DSM*'s classification system and the ADHD construct.

Additionally, the majority of individuals who exhibit ADHD behaviors also exhibit behavior found in other *DSM* disorders.[55] One example is oppositional-defiant disorder (ODD), which is diagnosed in approximately half of ADHD children.[56] Since secularists closely link ADHD and ODD, it is possible that these constructs are not separate, but part of a bigger problem the *DSM* committee and secularism has overlooked or even denied. According to some therapists, this subjective inclusion and exclusion of behaviors limits not only definitions but also assistance to individuals. For example, Robert Moss takes issue with not only limiting the definition of ADHD symptoms, but also in classifying these criteria as a disorder.

> The term "disorder" implies that this is a disease with specifically defined characteristics that appear in every case. ADD does not have a list of distinct symptoms that will be

[53] Ibid., 35.

[54] Hallowell and Ratey, *Driven to Distraction*, 9.

[55] Elissa P. Benedek, review of *ADHD in Adults: What the Science Says*, by Russell A. Barkley, Kevin Murphy, and Mariellen Fischer, *Bulletin of the Menninger Clinic* 73, no. 1 (Winter 2009): 69-74. The *DSM* provides what it refers to as *Differential Diagnoses* in which other disorders such as low self-esteem, anxiety disorders, conduct disorders, obsessive compulsive disorder, and or substance abuse are allegedly considered prior to the clinician assigning the diagnosis of ADHD to a child or adult (*DSM*, 87-89).

[56] *DSM*, 88; *NoSC*, 307.

present with each child. As we have seen, this condition encompasses a broad range of manifestations, and no two patients exhibit the same exact characteristics.[57]

Psychiatrists rationalize the inclusion and exclusion of behavior through comorbidity,[58] which allows them to diagnose children with unlimited numbers of disorders in order to describe fully all maladaptive behavior. Some children are diagnosed with multiple disorders at a time and prescribed medication for each.

Since the *DSM* is overwhelmingly subjective and therefore lacks validity, therapists must diagnose children based on subjective hypotheses that attempt to explain behaviors.[59] This realization led Thomas Insel, the Director of the National Institute of Mental Health (NIMH), to withdraw support for future revisions of the *DSM*: "The weakness [of the *DSM*] is its lack of validity. Unlike our definitions of ischemic heart disease, lymphoma, or AIDS, the *DSM* diagnoses are based on a consensus about clusters of clinical symptoms, not any objective laboratory measure."[60] In place of the *DSM*, the NIMH is proposing a more biological and empirical approach to mental disorders, which they call "Research Domain Criteria (RDoC)."[61] Still, secularists are already questioning

---

[57] Robert Moss, *Why Johnny Can't Concentrate: Coping with Attention Deficit Problems* (New York: Bantam, 1990), 3.

[58] Gabrielle Weiss and Lily Trokenberg Hechtman, *Hyperactive Children Grown Up: ADHD in Children, Adolescents, and Adults*, 2nd ed. (New York: Guilford, 1993), 346.

[59] *NoSC*, vii-viii.

[60] Thomas Insel, "Transforming Diagnosis"; available from http://www.nimh.nih.gov/about/director/2013/transforming-diagnosis.shtml; Internet.

[61] Ibid.

the validity of this newly proposed system of measurement.[62] Evidence simply does not exist by which secularists can empirically claim ADHD as a valid construct or a disease,[63] yet psychiatrists continue to push new theories to justify their hypotheses. Barkley, for example, views psychology's lack of a perfect theory and evidence of ADHD as both expected and legitimate.

> Since we ask not for perfection [in ADHD theory], but utility, we seek to build a ship that can be floated to be tested and revised, enabling us to build an even better ship that can be floated, tested, revised, and so on. Theories, like all accumulated information, are Darwinian in nature, evolving as their conceptual feet are held to empirical fires of experimentation, falsifiability, and revision.[64]

His statement implies that a practical theory of ADHD is acceptable even when it is not completely true. This pragmatic thinking encourages subjective faith in man's vacillating opinion rather than acceptance of objective scientific fact and immutable truth.

Further compromising the legitimacy of the diagnostic process and really undermining the entire ADHD construct presented in the *DSM* is the fourth type of ADHD listed in the *DSM* as "ADHD Not Otherwise Specified"[65] and defined in one sentence: "This category is for disorders with prominent symptoms of inattention or hyperactivity-impulsivity that do not meet criteria for ADHD."[66] While the *DSM* states that the criteria must be met for proper diagnoses to be

---

[62] Christopher Lane, "The NIMH Withdrawals Support for the DSM-5"; available from http://www.psychologytoday.com/blog/side-effects/201305/the-nimh-withdraws-support-dsm-5; Internet.

[63] David Stein, 22-23.

[64] *NoSC*, 361.

[65] *DSM*, 93.

[66] Ibid.

20

made, this description provides a catch-all subtype for what clinicians might feel fits their idea of the disorder. With the exception of behavior (inattention, hyperactivity, or impulsivity), the "Not Otherwise Specified" subtype eliminates all previous criteria as the basis for diagnosing ADHD and establishes the therapist's subjective opinion as the true system of measurement for ADHD.

This subjective expectation has led some well-respected psychiatrists to popularize the idea that not all ADHD behaviors are observable. Since psychiatry bases the diagnostic process and the *DSM* criteria on observable behavior,[67] the claim of non-detectable symptoms suggests that non-*DSM* criteria exist for ADHD:

> ADD comes in many shapes and sizes. In many people, particularly adults, the symptoms of ADD are masked by more obvious problems such as depression or gambling or drinking, and the underlying ADD is never detected. In other people the symptoms take on a particular cast, congruent with the person's personality as it evolves over time, so that the symptoms are never really noticed the way symptoms of a cold or flu might be but rather are dismissed as being part of 'just the way he is,' not warranting medical or psychiatric intervention. And within the domain of properly diagnosed ADD, there is also much variability.[68]

Their suggestion not only reveals the subjective nature of the diagnostic process, but clearly defines ADHD as an abstract idea that may be unobservable. This characterization of the construct is produced by the "not otherwise specified" subtype and further undermines both the *DSM's* and ADHD construct's validity and reliability.

---

[67] Ibid., 92.

[68] Hallowell and Ratey, *Driven to Distraction*, 9.

The History of the ADHD Label

A Moral Beginning

Throughout its brief history, the various labels for the behaviors known today as ADHD have reflected the social views of their time. Physician George Still designated the first label used to identify these behaviors in children in 1902 as "a morbid defect in moral control."[69] Still explained the label as representing children who were "aggressive, passionate, lawless, inattentive, impulsive, and overactive."[70] Though secular therapists generally view this nomenclature as puritanical,[71] the label accurately describes society's view in the early 1900s that all behavior was moral,[72] a view which is in line with Scripture. The original label — morbid defect in moral control — describes well the fallen condition of all people without Christ (depravity) and not just a small percentage of children who exhibit unacceptable behavior. Scripture tells us that we are all naturally dead (morbid) in our trespasses and sins (heart conditions and behaviors; Eph 2:1). Since we are all in sin, we are defective or imperfect. This lack of holiness/perfection is moral in nature, and without the control of the Holy Spirit, we cannot meet God's moral standard and please Him. Romans 8:1-17 offers us the only antidote to our morbid defect in moral control –it is the work of God the

---

[69] George Still, "Some Abnormal Physical Conditions in Children," *Lancet Medical Journal* (1902): 1009.

[70] *NoSC*, 4.

[71] Hallowell and Ratey, *Driven to Distraction,* 166.

[72] Lloyd, Kameenui, and Chard, 30.

Father, Son, and Holy Spirit that gives us life and moral control, which allows us to please God and behave accordingly. Unlike secularists, however, Scripture focuses on the whole man (spiritual and physical natures) and not merely on the behaviors.

Twenty years later after the first label, psychiatrists changed the label to "post-encephalitic behaviors disorder."[73] This change revealed the shift in how psychiatrists and society viewed and approached behavior[74] through biology and specifically neurology rather than through moral anthropology. Hallowell and Ratey explain this sentiment:

> Where the story began is impossible to say. Certainly, the symptoms of ADD have been with us as long as history has been recorded. However, the modern story of ADD, the story of bringing those symptoms out of the realm of morality and punishment and into the realm of science and treatment, began somewhere around the turn of the century.[75]

They go on to write, "As clinicians began to speculate that neurology, rather than the devil, was governing behavior, a kinder, more effective approach to child-rearing emerged."[76] In 1960, the third label "minimal brain dysfunction"[77] was

---

[73] Encephalitis is brain inflammation caused by viral infection.

[74] Peter Gray, "The 'ADHD Personality': Its Cognitive, Biological, and Evolutionary Foundations"; available from http://www.psychologytoday.com/blog/freedom-learn/201008/the-adhd-personality-its-cognitive-biological-and-evolutionary-foundations; Internet.

[75] Edward M. Hallowell and John J. Ratey, *Driven to Distraction: Recognizing and Coping with Attention Deficit Disorder from Childhood through Adulthood* (New York: Pantheon Books, 1994), 270.

[76] Ibid, 272.

[77] Lloyd, Kameenui, and Chard, 31.

assigned to ADHD behaviors and remained consistent with the psychiatric view that behavior is amoral[78] and biologically caused:

> We have been led down a slippery slope of labels. What used to be called appropriately and simply a behavioral problem or difficulty came to be a labeled a 'behavioral disorder.' 'Disorders' are not very different from, or a result of, 'diseases.' Almost overnight, simple behavior problems became 'brain diseases.'[79]

In 1968 the label changed once again to "developmental hyperactivity" and "hyperkinetic reaction."[80] These labels formed the basis of the label assigned in 1980 as "attention-deficit disorder." [81] Even today, some still refer to ADHD as ADD.

As with the ADHD criteria, society and psychotherapy in particular rely on the *DSM* to provide a common working label and a common language to describe the ADHD construct. Secularists often think of the *DSM* as the bible of psychopathology; however, the NIMH sees it for what it is: "a dictionary, creating a set of labels and defining each."[82] ADHD, then, is a label: valuable in revealing secularist's anthropology and moral views rather than valuable in defining a child.

---

[78] Barkley defines morality as a measurement of acceptable behavior as it relates to oneself (*NoSC*, 179-80). However, the Bible teaches that God judges man's thoughts, motives, and behaviors in relation to his holy character (1 Pet 1:13-17). Secularists still use the word *morality* in their writing but their understanding of morality excludes any reference to God.

[79] Flora, 14.

[80] David Benner, ed., *Encyclopedia of Psychology* (Grand Rapids: Baker, 1985), 80.

[81] Haber, 30.

[82] Thomas Insel, "Transforming Diagnosis."

A Controversial Existence

The current label of ADHD is not without controversy even among secular therapists. Barkley, whom many consider to be the foremost authority on the ADHD construct, suggests the current label reflects a problem of attention and hyperactivity,[83] but he dismisses ADHD as a deficit in attention and instead describes the condition as a "deficit in inhibition." Barkley asserts, "This new theory suggests that the problems with inattention are due to a biological inability to regulate inhibition. This deficit in inhibition in turn has a harmful effect on the brain's executive functions, causing poor self-guidance and self-regulation of behavioral information."[84] His newest theory suggests that ADHD is not the best label to describe the maladaptive behaviors listed in the *DSM*: "For at least the past 18 of 30 years, pride of place among these three symptoms has gone to inattention as the chief characteristic of this disorder. . . . This view of ADHD is no longer scientifically defensible."[85] Many psychotherapists agree with Barkley that ADHD is no longer the best choice of labels to accurately describe these behaviors. For example, Moss takes issue with the term *hyperactivity* since "most ADD children are not hyperactive."[86] Still other secular therapists show concern with labeling these behaviors as a disorder,[87] while a

---

[83] Russell A. Barkley, "Shift in Perspective Offers Insights into Biological Nature of ADHD," *AAP News* 15, no. 3 (1999): 38.

[84] Ibid.

[85] *NoSC*, 313.

[86] Moss, 3.

[87] Ibid.

number of experts believe the label should emphasize "an interest deficit," since those labeled ADHD are able to pay attention to things that interest them most.

> According to the theory, the trouble is a lack of motivation as well as a deficit of attention: People with the disorder can't generate the same degree of enthusiasm as other people for activities they don't automatically find appealing. "Parents always wonder why their children with ADHD can skateboard for hours and practice the same thing over and over but can't stay on task in school," said Swanson, who said he and fellow researchers have taken to calling the syndrome "an interest deficit."[88]

In a similar manner, the *DSM* also identifies a child's interest as dictating his behavior:

> Symptoms typically worsen in situations that require sustained attention or mental effort or that lack intrinsic appeal or novelty (e.g., listening to classroom teachers, doing class assignments, listening to or reading lengthy materials, or working on monotonous, repetitive tasks). Signs of the disorder may be minimal or absent when the person is receiving frequent rewards for appropriate behavior, is under close supervision, is in a novel setting, is engaged in especially interesting activities, is in a one-to-one situation (e.g., the clinician's office).[89]

This *DSM* qualification describes normal human behavior and undermines the current theory that ADHD is "a deficit involving response inhibition."[90] Instead, the *DSM* and many clinicians describe ADHD as a lack of desire and motivation. Though Barkley does not endorse *desire* as a key theoretical term, he is quoted often as stating, "There is no ADD while playing Nintendo."[91] Many children labeled ADHD can sit still during video games, remain quiet during their favorite movies, and participate in recreation for hours upon end without losing focus. Furthermore the *DSM*'s claim that "signs of the disorder may be minimal

---

[88] Ellison, "Brain Scans."

[89] *DSM*, 86-87.

[90] *NoSC*, 65.

[91] Hallowell and Ratey, *Driven to Distraction*, 280.

or absent when the person is under close supervision"[92] exposes that an "attention deficiency" is really misplaced focus.

Barkley proposes that ADHD children lack necessary control over their behavior.[93] With this claim, Barkley, perhaps unwittingly, brings the ADHD community full circle to the original label of "morbid defect in moral control." The only difference is the exclusion of morality in the current model, which Pennington observes: "Although these terms [*volitional inhibition* and a *defect in moral control*] sound quaint to our modern ears, they capture the idea that motivation is inevitably an important input to the process of response selection."[94] Instead of early labels that reveal the moral nature of behavior, Barkley suggests a new label, "developmental disorder of self-control,"[95] to better reflect the current theories. All agree that ADHD is not the best label to describe children's maladaptive behaviors.

It is important to note the nomenclature of the ADHD construct may continue to change as it reflects the changing anthropological views of secular society. Studying the various labels reveals both the current labels' subjectivity as well as the historical trend away from the biblical moral view of man. So what does this mean we should do with the created secular label? Since the ADHD label lacks clarity in identifying the source of ADHD behavior, and since it falsely places children in a hopeless situation, we must refuse to embrace the

---

[92] *DSM*, 86-87.

[93] *NoSC*, viii.

[94] Pennington, 162.

[95] *TCoA*, 61.

secular label and instead place our faith in objective scriptural perspectives on these same behaviors, which will both reveal their cause and provide our children with the historically proven remedy.

The Secular Theories of ADHD Etiology

In addition to understanding the labeling process, those dealing with this label must also be aware of secular psychology's theories of ADHD etiology, that is, the causes of the alleged disorder. Currently, psychotherapy has only etiological hypotheses for their construct since "the precise causes of ADHD are unknown."[96] Though secularists have yet to validate a cause to ADHD, they speculate about three "potentially causative factors"[97]: (1) abnormal brains, (2) chemically imbalanced brains[98] and (3) genetic flaws.[99]

Abnormal Brains

Seemingly substantial theories suggest that ADHD is caused by abnormal brains in those labeled ADHD. These claims are based on results of neuroimaging of ADHD brains compared to those of so-called normal individuals. Though psychotherapy has widely accepted this research as hard evidence for ADHD etiology, researchers admit that these studies do "not prove that ADHD arises from these particular brain structures."[100] More specifically,

---

[96] *NoSC*, 29.

[97] Ibid.

[98] Monastra, 29.

[99] *NoSC*, 37.

[100] Ibid., 35.

secularists view chemical imbalances in the brain (dopamine and serotonin) and a smaller prefrontal cortex as providing the strongest evidence to support this hypothesis.[101] Though researchers and pharmaceutical companies have conducted thousands of studies attempting to prove their etiological hypotheses,[102] no solid empirical evidence exists to validate their claims.[103] Furthermore, many researchers arrive at different conclusions about the same studies:

> The study, which appeared in the proceedings of the National Academy of Sciences, used medical imaging techniques to examine the brains of children with and without ADHD symptoms. Researchers did not find any permanent flaws or deficits in the brains of the ADHD children, but did discover that parts of the ADHD children's brains were developing more slowly than those of other children . . . Dr. Philip Shaw told the *New York Times* (11-13-07), "I think this is pretty strong evidence we're talking about a delay, and not an abnormal brain."[104]

Not only do the current neurological studies fail to prove causality of differentials in both brain development and brain size, but the studies are also replete with invalidating factors. One such invalidating factor is the presence of stimulant medications in the children tested:

> Neuroscientists have made much-touted progress in understanding the brain, but still that understanding is extremely superficial. We have no idea, really, how the brain does any of the amazing things it does (beyond the simplest reflexes), but we do have some ideas about which parts of the brain are most involved in which functions. . . . Not surprisingly, therefore, researchers looking for brain correlates of ADHD have focused on the prefrontal cortex and on dopamine. The results of such research are highly variable from lab to lab, with much controversy resulting. Also, the results are often confounded because most of the people in the ADHD groups have been treated with stimulant drugs, either at the time of study or in the past, so it is not clear if any brain

---

[101] Gray, "ADHD Personality."

[102] *NoSC*, 29-46.

[103] Petersen, 106.

[104] Education Reporter, *Newspaper of Education Rights* no. 263 (Dec. 2007): 1.

difference observed is a correlate of the ADHD itself or is caused by long-term effects of the drug.[105]

Gray further explains that psychotropic drugs affect both the physicality of the brain and the results of the studies[106] and concludes his findings by stating,

> So far no biological marker of ADHD has been found that is sufficiently reliable to be used as an aid in diagnosis. The studies of brain differences are interesting, but they have no bearing at all on the question of whether ADHD is a disorder or a normal personality variation. All personality variations have a basis in the brain. Of course they do. The brain controls all of behavior, so any difference that is reflected in behavior must exist in the brain.[107]

Brain scans do not prove ADHD's existence, but rather they provide evidence that all behavior somehow originates in the brain[108] — a point on which all sides agree. Renowned pediatrician William Carey also sees the lack of empirical guidelines in research as a problem that must be addressed in order to validate claims that ADHD is caused by brain malfunctions. He insists that there exists "an absence of clear evidence that the ADHD symptoms are related to brain malfunction. . . . Chemical testing and brain imaging techniques have not proven anything. The associations demonstrated so far have been inconsistent and are not clear as to cause, association, or consequence of the symptoms."[109] Though

---

[105] Gray, "ADHD Personality."

[106] Similar studies show that Ritalin physically alters rats' brains (Menhard, 53).

[107] Gray, "ADHD Personality."

[108] For further study about how EEGs and other brain scans do not validate the ADHD construct or prove an ADHD diagnosis, see Daniel Berger II, *Teaching a Child to Pay Attention: Proverbs 4:20-27* (Taylors, S.C.: Alethia International Publications, 2015). For further study about the brain and behaviors from a Christian worldview, see Ed Welch, *Blame it on the Brain? Distinguishing Chemical Imbalances, Brain Disorders, and Disobedience* (Phillipsburg, N.J.: Presbyterian and Reformed, 1998).

[109] "What to Do about the ADHD Epidemic," *American Academy of Pediatrics: Developmental and Behavioral Pediatrics Newsletter* (Autumn 2003): 6-7; available from http://www.ahrp.org/children/CareyADHD0603.php; Internet.

scientists search for biological answers in neurochemistry, many clinicians acknowledge that being human consists of more than mere measureable chemicals.[110] Alvin Poussaint, professor of psychiatry at Harvard University, bluntly admits, "I don't think anything is ever going to be strictly biological that has to do with the brain."[111] Confessions such as these expose that man is more than a biological animal and that his behaviors are more than a product of brainwaves, which can be pharmaceutically adjusted.

Chemical Imbalances

The other claim associated with neuropsychology is that ADHD is caused by a chemical imbalance. This popular secular theory is based on the cause/effect principle; as Wender notes: "Medication can be regarded as a form of replacement therapy; that is, it *apparently* [emphasis added] supplies chemicals that are lacking or causes the body to create more of the missing chemicals. "[112] This presumed chemical imbalance is also the major argument for why secularists consider psychotropic drugs necessary to treat ADHD.[113] Wender explains the logic they use to arrive at this conclusion: "The widespread effect of stimulant medication on various psychological functions has led child

---

[110] Stephen Post in *Generation RX*, DVD, directed by Kevin P. Miller (Vancouver: Common Radius Films, 2008), 5:40.

[111] *Generation RX*, 5:07.

[112] Wender, *ADHD*, 69; Paul Wender is known as the "Dean of ADHD," since he was one of the first psychiatrists (in 1971) to theorize that the child's maladaptive behaviors were genetically caused. "Biography"; available from http://www.webmd.com/paul-h-wender; Internet.

[113] Wender, *ADHD*, 65.

psychiatrists to believe that the brain chemistry of people with ADHD is in some ways different from that of others."[114]

Though psychotherapy asserts that chemical imbalance is a valid etiology, their lack of empirical evidence and the complexity of the brain reveal secularist's theory to be an unproven hypothesis. Just as secularism applies a non-existent standard of development to each diagnosis of ADHD, it also applies a non-existent standard of chemical levels in the brain (i.e., "chemical imbalances," specifically in the neurotransmitters) as a potential etiology of ADHD. Not only do chemical levels differ between individuals, rendering a standard level of each brain chemical impossible, but chemicals also fluctuate at high levels in each individual (between different emotions, activities, and mental processes) and make so-called normal levels of brain chemicals immeasurable.[115] These differences make the determination of a set standard of normal chemical balance impossible and in turn invalidate the etiological claim of chemical imbalances. David Burns of Stanford University, as quoted by Petersen, stresses that "we cannot measure brain serotonin levels in living human beings, so there is no way to test this theory. Some neuroscientists would question whether the theory of chemical imbalance is even viable, since the brain does not function in this way, as a hydraulic system."[116] In the documentary *Generation RX*, renowned psychiatrist Peter Breggin also reveals his concern with psychiatry's claim of chemical imbalance.

---

[114] Ibid., 72-75.

[115] Rosemond and Ravenel, 64-65.

[116] Petersen, 105.

> It's quite ironic actually, because the only imbalances that we know of in the brains of people called mental patients are the ones inflicted on them by the psychiatric drugs. How ironic: we make a false claim that they have chemical imbalances and then we give them chemical imbalances.[117]

Doctors and scientists simply cannot know when a chemical is imbalanced, yet ADHD advocates strongly assert they do.

Abnormal Chromosomes (Genetic)

Besides the etiological claims of neurology, there also exists the popular genetic claim.[118] Though Barkley leads the way in pronouncing ADHD to be both neurological and genetic, he also acknowledges that "far more research is needed before we can be as sanguine about the biological nature of ADHD as we might like to be."[119] He further admits that "no evidence exists to show that ADHD is the result of abnormal chromosomal structures," yet he dogmatically states that heredity is a validated etiology for ADHD.[120] In spite of researchers' failure to discover the ADHD gene or chromosome, psychiatrists are sure it exists.

Alternative Theories

In addition to these widely held hypotheses, less-accepted theories of ADHD etiology also exist. These include dietary causes,[121] exposure to lead at an

---

[117] *Generation RX*, 7:10.

[118] Monastra, 39.

[119] *NoSC*, 32.

[120] Ibid., 37.

[121] Fletcher-Janzen and Reynolds, 74.

early age,[122] maternal smoking,[123] sensory stimulants (e.g., excessive TV viewing),[124] premature births,[125] and theories such as "symmetric tonic neck reflex."[126] The reality that all children by nature need the attention and supervision of authority has led the Breggins to use the label "DADD"[127] (dad attention deficit disorder) to illustrate their years of clinical observation. They are convinced that ADHD behavior is a result of a father's failure to give his child necessary attention.[128] Still other clinicians hold that ADHD is a problem not with children but with the current education system in which they are placed.[129]

The *DSM* acknowledges that a history of child abuse, drug exposure, lead poisoning, infections, low birth weight, or even mental retardation could all be present in these children's lives, yet the *DSM* does not hold that these conditions

---

[122] J.M. Braun et al., "Exposures to Environmental Toxicants and Attention Deficit Hyperactivity Disorder in U.S. Children," *Environmental Health Perspectives* 12 (December 2006): 14.

[123] "Bad Behavior 'Linked to Smoking,'" BBC News; available from http://news.bbc.co.uk/2/hi/health/4727197.stm; Internet.

[124] Robin Weiss, "Babies and TV"; available from http://pregnancy.about.com/od/ourbaby/a/babiesandtv.htm; Internet.

[125] Christian Nordqvist, "Premature Babies Much More Likely to Have ADHD"; available from http://www.medicalnewstoday.com/articles/44574.php; Internet; accessed 18 September 2010.

[126] Nancy E. O'Dell and Patricia A. Cook, *Stopping ADHD: A Unique and Proven Drug-Free Program for Treating ADHD Children and Adults* (New York: Avery Publishers, 2004). Their entire book proposes a theory which states that children who did not learn to crawl lack control over their bodies and behaviors, and thus ADHD is the result. This theory promotes a form of secular behavior modification.

[127] Breggin and Breggin, 55-72.

[128] Ibid.

[129] Moss, 129.

cause ADHD. Psychiatry's claim to know what does not cause ADHD (environmental issues, medical issues, diets, sleep patterns, etc.)[130] implies that secularists are sure of its cause, yet clinicians admit that empirical evidence to prove ADHD etiology still eludes them.[131]

> The exact mechanism underlying ADD remains unknown. There is no single lesion of the brain, no single neurotransmitter system, no single gene we have identified that triggers ADD. The precise workings of the brain that underlie ADD have so far escaped us, in part due to the extraordinary complexity of the attentional system.[132]

Scientists must continue to search for causes of maladaptive behavior,[133] since many believe that justification of the construct's continued existence depends on this discovery — or at least the never-ending search to make the construct appear scientific.

The Secular Treatments for ADHD

Because psychotherapy argues that ADHD is neurologically and biologically caused, it stands to reason that their proposed treatments are also rooted in neurology and biology. While secularists accept and use prescription drugs, behavior modification, and alternative means of treating ADHD, they admit that no current treatment provides an actual cure. Instead, clinicians assign treatment plans aiming to help those diagnosed with ADHD to better cope in life and enhance academic performance.[134]

---

[130] Ibid.

[131] *NoSC,* 29.

[132] Hallowell and Ratey, *Driven to Distraction,* 269.

[133] *NoSC,* 37-41.

[134] Hallowell and Ratey, *Driven to Distraction,* 235.

Prescription Medication

Many clinicians not only consider psychotropic drugs to be a sensible part of treating ADHD, but medications represent the most common and often the only form of treatment.[135] Though secularists attest that medications are not a cure for a child's problems,[136] they do provide three seemingly beneficial outcomes. The first benefit of medicating children who are said to have ADHD is that doing so typically calms the child. Besides the calming effect of stimulants, another outcome of prescribed stimulant medications such as Ritalin and Adderall is increased focus.[137] The ability to focus attention along with the decrease in hyperactivity allows for the most desired benefit of medications: allegedly better behavioral performances in school and at home.[138]

As beneficial as these appear, the question of validity and adverse effects remains. Rosemond and Ravenel point out that stimulant medication has "the same effect on both the hyperactive child and the non-hyperactive individual."[139] These drugs provide each consumer with a direct effect on the central nervous system that incites mood and behavior, increases mental focus, and can heighten the rate of productivity.[140] These common effects of stimulants not only raise

---

[135] In 2012, nearly five million people had prescriptions filled for ADHD medications. "Report: Turning Attention to ADHD"; available from http://lab.express-scripts.com/insights/industry-updates/report-turning-attention-to-adhd; Internet; accessed 12 March 2014.

[136] Hallowell and Ratey, *Driven to Distraction*, 235.

[137] Weiss and Hechtman, 349.

[138] Gray, "ADHD Personality."

[139] Rosemond and Ravenel, 92.

[140] Flora, 3-4.

questions as to how psychotropic drugs treat ADHD, but they also explain why ADHD medications are so widely abused. Though ADHD medications may stimulate the nervous system and result in more desirable behavior, [141] stimulants do not treat or cure ADHD.[142]

Another concern about the use of these schedule 2 stimulants[143] is their side effects. Debate over the unknown long-term effects of stimulant drugs to treat ADHD permeates discussions.[144] Some studies show that stimulant medications are completely safe,[145] while other studies point to deaths, severe headaches, sleep disturbance,[146] stunted growth, weight loss, addictions,[147] depression,[148] psychotic behavior,[149] and suicide.[150] Breggin and other

---

[141] Ibid., 77.

[142] Weiss and Hechtman, 366; Flora, 4.

[143] "Drug Scheduling." Available from http://www.justice.gov/dea/druginfo/ds.shtml; Internet.

[144] Menhard, 67.

[145] Wender, *ADHD*, 82-83.

[146] Saul, 28-32.

[147] Though ADHD advocates argue that the stimulants given to those labeled ADHD are not addictive, they do admit that "there is potential for abuse and addiction with any stimulant medication." WebMD, "Stimulant Drugs for ADHD"; available from http://www.webmd.com/add-adhd/guide/adhd-stimulant-therapy; Internet; accessed 10 July 2011.

[148] Ibid.

[149] Weiss and Hechtman, 352-57.

[150] Saul, 29.

clinicians[151] have concluded that stimulant medications create serious concerns rather than benefits: "Medications for everything from depression and anxiety to ADHD and insomnia are being prescribed in alarming numbers across the country, but the 'cure' is often worse than the original problem."[152] The Drug Enforcement Administration states of schedule 2 drugs (of which Adderall and Ritalin are listed),

> Schedule II drugs, substances, or chemicals are defined as drugs with a high potential for abuse, less abuse potential than Schedule I drugs, with use potentially leading to severe psychological or physical dependence. *These drugs are also considered dangerous* [emphasis added].[153]

Though not enough evidence exists to fully understand the effects of psychiatric drugs on children,[154] most professionals concur with this one idea: psychiatric drugs do not remedy a child's real problems.[155] Petersen asserts, "You can't just keep medicating people and medicating people and not deal with the underlying issue."[156] For this reason many professionals endorse and pursue alternatives to medication for treating ADHD.

---

[151] Ibid., xiii-xviii.

[152] Peter Breggin, "Medication Madness: The Role of Psychiatric Drugs in Cases of Violence, Suicide and Murder"; available from http://www.breggin.com/index.php?option=com_content&task=view&id=55&Itemid=79; Internet.

[153] "Drug Scheduling." Available from http://www.justice.gov/dea/druginfo/ds.html; Internet.

[154] Ibid.

[155] Most clinicians admit that psychotropic drugs only help children (and their families) cope with their condition rather than remedy their problem.

[156] Petersen, 95.

38

Behavior Modification

Many psychotherapists use behavior modification, also known as behaviorism or behavioral therapy, along with drug therapy, although many view behavior modification as only an alternative to drug therapy. Behaviorists view behavior as the main problem, the source of the problem, and the focus of remedy.[157] The primary emphasis of behavior modification is the biological nature of man that ignores man's immaterial existence, though most behaviorists argue that clinicians should consider thinking and feeling to be behaviors also.[158]

The basic treatment for ADHD that behavioral therapy implements is a "carefully planned use of rewards and punishments for eliminating undesirable behavior or establishing desirable behavior or both."[159] This therapy also sees structured activities such as daily exercise, eating properly, adequate rest, and other positive activities as improving performance and overall quality of life. According to behaviorists, your behavior is not to blame for your children's behavior, though they will just as quickly inform you that you likewise need your behavior modified.[160] Though behavior modification can improve a child's outward behavior, it fails to address the heart as the true source of all behavior and as it relates to pleasing God.

---

[157] Weiss and Hechtman, 367.

[158] Flora, 21.

[159] O'Dell and Cook, 38.

[160] Weiss and Hechtman, 366.

Alternative Treatments

Alternative treatments, such as dietary[161] and herbal treatments,[162] are also sometimes proposed by therapists. No side of the ADHD issue rejects the notion that food affects behavior and performance, but food is not the cause or the solution to behavior. Others promote alternative treatments such as "symmetric tonic neck reflex," in which children are taught body control through crawling and holding positions.[163] These approaches to treating ADHD share the belief that ADHD is a physical disorder with a physical solution.

While some clinicians argue that ADHD is caused by video games and excessive television,[164] others argue that video games provide a valid remedy that can "train people to make the right decisions faster."[165] This newly proposed treatment is "designed to affect the prefrontal cortex-behavior-and visual and motor parts of the brain and strengthen the ability to concentrate and to ignore distractions."[166] Yet, the proposition that the ADHD brain can be taught to pay attention undermines current theories, and thus secularists usually reject it.

---

[161] Monastra, 75-91.

[162] Haber, 137-52.

[163] O'Dell and Cook, 13-32.

[164] Weiss, "Babies and TV."

[165] Brian Gormley, "Can Videogames Treat ADHD?: Start-Ups Seek FDA Approval for Games That Help Attention Disorders," *Wall Street Journal*, Tuesday, July 31, 2012, B6.

[166] Ibid.

Conclusion

The evidence clearly shows that the ADHD diagnosis is merely a subjective construct that secularists have created to deal with children's behavioral problems. Though their theories are widespread, they have yet to identify valid causes, objective testing, or proven remedies to children's behavioral problems let alone their spiritual needs. Instead of trusting in this subjective construct of secularism, parents and counselors must turn to the reliable and proven wisdom of God's Word, which offers valid answers and genuine hope.

CHAPTER 2 – ADDRESSING BAD BEHAVIOR

The alternative to the ever-changing secular perspective of children's behavior is the Scripture's proven perspective. Though behaviors are not the foundational problem, they are observable manifestations of the child's core problem that must be addressed. Scripture speaks about behavior at length, and it specifically addresses most of the criteria that secularists describe as ADHD.

Understand the Presuppositions

In order to deal with the child's behaviors effectively, one must first understand the underlying presuppositions behind all theories of behavior. Though many secularists prefer to present the ADHD construct as a matter of science, all approaches to the diagnosis of ADHD and to human behavior in general require an anthropological presupposition. In other words, all views of ADHD—secular or religious—require faith. Even Barkley himself, perhaps unknowingly, supports this truth:

> Any theory of child psychopathological condition such as ADHD will ultimately have to be linked to larger theories of the nature of normal developmental psychological processes and the neuropsychological processes that comprise them. . . . Consequently, any theory of ADHD is, of necessity, a theory of executive functions and self-regulation.[1]

---

[1] Russell A. Barkley, *ADHD and the Nature of Self-Control* (New York: Guilford, 2005), vii-'iii. Hereafter referred to as *NoSC*.

41

Though Barkley emphasizes his own secular theory and coined terms, his proposition exposes a larger foundational issue to every approach to the ADHD label and to self-control: one's view of the concept of ADHD (abnormality) is born out of his philosophical view of human nature (normality). Therefore, the most profitable and necessary discussion concerning ADHD etiology is the discussion of the origin and nature of man that explains his behaviors (see appendix A).

ADHD Behaviors from a Secular Presupposition

Secular theories about ADHD presuppose the theory of evolution.[2] Barkley's admitted belief in evolution typifies the secular underpinning of ADHD and explains secularists' approaches to man's problems. As worldviews changed at the turn of the twentieth century from aligned biblical views to more distinct secular perspectives, so followed psychological theories and practices of caring for the souls of men:

> [Man] was now seen as being part of the natural order, different from non-human animals only in degree of structural complexity. This made it possible and plausible, for the first time, to treat man as an object of scientific investigation, and to conceive of the vast and varied range of human behavior, and the motivational causes from which it springs, as being amenable in principle to scientific explanation. Much of the creative work done in a whole variety of diverse scientific fields over the next century was to be inspired by, and derive sustenance from, this new world-view.[3]

---

[2] For further reading on Barkley's evolutionary beliefs and subsequent theories, see Russell A. Barkley, *Executive Functions: What They Are, How They Work, and Why They Evolved* (New York: Guilford, 2012).

[3] "Sigmund Freud (1856-1939)"; available from http://www.iep.utm.edu/freud/#H2; Internet; accessed 21 April 2014. Brownback writes, "Science will solve the problems of want and illness, and psychology and sociology will care for man's internal and external behavioral problems" (*The Danger of Self Love: Re-examining a Popular Myth* [Chicago: Moody, 1982], 29).

This proposition also explains why the ADHD construct is so widely accepted in American culture and even influential in many churches.[4] In spite of the reality that secular psychology explains, diagnoses, and treats human behaviors from the presupposition that man is an evolved animal,[5] many believers choose to accept their proposed theories of anthropology and subsequent theories of behavior.

So what do secularists believe about the nature of children they diagnose as having ADHD? Secularists view normal children as amoral beings born with the ability "to be organized, planful [*sic*], and goal-directed,"[6] and they view children who are diagnosed with ADHD as having a problem that inhibits them from self-control, faith in future reward, and the ability to make right choices.[7] Barkley describes this premise as

> a disturbance in a child's ability to inhibit immediate reactions to the moment so as to use self-control with regard to time and future. . . . What is not developing properly in your child is the capacity to shift from focusing on the here and now to focusing on the future. When all a child focuses on is the moment, acting impulsively makes sense. From the child's perspective, it is always "now." But this can be disastrous when the child is expected to be developing a focus on what lies ahead and what needs to be done to meet the future effectively.[8]

---

[4] "Not only have [Christians] embraced humanism's values and suffered its symptoms, but we have gone a step further. We have accepted humanism's diagnosis of what ails the human soul and have eagerly begun to practice the 'cure' it prescribes. Nowhere is this more evident than in the presuppositions and counseling methodology of 'Christian' psychology" (Jim Owen, *Christian Psychology's War on God's Word: The Victimization of the Believer* [Stanley, N.C.: Timeless Texts, 2003], 17).

[5] Edward M. Hallowell and John J. Ratey, *Driven to Distraction: Recognizing and Coping with Attention Deficit Disorder* (New York: Pantheon Books, 1994), 270.

[6] Russell A. Barkley, *Taking Charge of ADHD: A Complete Authoritative Guide for Parents.* rev. ed. (New York: Guilford, 2000), xi. Hereafter referred to as *TCoA*.

[7] Ibid.

[8] Ibid.

Barkley's hypothesis of the nature of self-control in a child diagnosed as ADHD describes the natural heart of every man that lacks self-control and desires immediate gratification over future rewards. If his premise were accurate, then children diagnosed with ADHD would theoretically be incapable of ever having faith in God. Scripture, however, describes all men as being incapable of having a right eternal mindset (faith), God-pleasing self-control, and freedom to behave rightly apart from God's grace and the Holy Spirit's work of illumination and regeneration (1 Cor 2:4-16). Rather than believing that a child is abnormal and has a disease, those who counsel must by faith view the child scripturally — as naturally depraved and in need of intimacy with Christ by grace through faith. As will be later discussed in this chapter, the scriptural position of man does not deny that valid physical problems can also affect a child's behaviors, since man is psychosomatic in nature. Physical problems, however, never cause alleged ADHD.

Not only is the evolutionary theory the presupposition for the secular ADHD label, but the theory also governs the American educational system where the ADHD construct flourishes.[9] Though John Dewey is best known as the father of progressive education, he was also a prominent psychologist and the eighth president of the APA who "felt the idea of God hindered creative intelligence."[10] America's acceptance of Dewey's ideologies in both education and psychology provided the ideal environment for the popularization of the

---

[9] Robert Moss, *Why Johnny Can't Concentrate: Coping with Attention Deficit Problems* (New York: Bantam, 1990), 129, 142.

[10] David Benner and Peter Hill, eds., *Baker Encyclopedia of Psychology and Counseling*, 2nd ed. (Grand Rapids: Baker, 1999), 347.

ADHD idea.[11] As God was removed from the home and the school (cultural places of learning), American education became humanistic and harmful. One direct result of removing God from the educational system is that the natural foolishness of the heart reveals itself in uninhibited foolish behavior: "The fool says in his heart, 'There is no God.' They are corrupt, they do abominable deeds, there is none who does good" (Ps 14:1).[12] If society refuses to acknowledge the reality of man's depraved nature and refuses to teach right theological presuppositions in places of learning, we should expect man's behavior to degenerate as it reflects man's rejection of God's goodness and creative wisdom.

Like Dewey and Barkley, psychotherapists in general reject the biblical doctrine of anthropology[13] and, instead, search for causes of behavior within the framework of neuroscience and the evolutionary theory.[14] Their conclusions exclude consideration of man's need of redemption in Christ and the marred image of God which exists in all men. Though secularists reject the gospel, they do understand that "effective treatment [of ADHD] often requires a radical

---

[11] Thomas S. Szasz, *Pharmacracy: Medicine and Politics in America* (New York: Praeger, 2001), 212; James J. Chriss, *Social Control: An Introduction* (Cambridge: Polity, 2007), 230.

[12] Clarke writes, "The corruption of their *hearts* extends itself through all the actions of their *lives*. . . . Not *one of them does good*. He cannot, for he has no Divine influence, and he denies that such can be received" (Adam Clarke, *Psalms*, electronic ed., Clarke's Commentaries [Albany, Ore.: Ages Software, 1999], Ps 14:1).

[13] Sigmund Freud, *Psychoanalysis and Faith* (New York: Basic Books, 1964), 104. ADHD is not the only secular label born out of the evolutionary theory and anthropocentric presuppositions.

[14] Peter Gray, "The 'ADHD Personality': Its Cognitive, Biological, and Evolutionary Foundations"; available from http://www.psychologytoday.com/blog/freedom-learn/201008/the-adhd-personality-its-cognitive-biological-and-evolutionary-foundations; internet.

rethinking of your view of yourself."[15] The most radical and necessary view, one which completely opposes man's natural estimation of himself, is Scripture's assessment of man.

ADHD Behaviors from a Biblical Presupposition

In contrast to the secular presupposition, the historical account of creation and how man relates to his Creator are presuppositions which must be set forth in homes, schools, and society in general and are the only presuppositions which lead to valid solutions. Scripture is clear about the depraved nature of all men. The book of Romans presents a concise anthropology that establishes God as Creator and the gospel as essential to the redemption of fallen man (1:16-23; 2:1-6:23). In the second portion of chapter 1, Paul refers to the Genesis account of how all men corporately became fools. In Romans 3:10-18, God pronounces man's behavior to be morally reprehensible and every man's heart to be self-serving rather than worshipping his Creator. As the natural man self-deceptively (Jer 17:9) views himself as wise, he foolishly trusts his own understanding and believes the same core deception found in Genesis 3:5 that the serpent falsely claimed would allow man "to be like God." Unlike man's deceptive opinion of himself, scriptural anthropology is God's wisdom, which precisely exposes the heart of every man (Jer 17:9-10).[16] Accepting God's view of human behavior does require humility, but doing so is foundational to addressing the source of the

---

[15] Edward M. Hallowell and John J. Ratey, *Driven to Distraction: Recognizing and Coping with Attention Deficit Disorder* (New York: Pantheon Books, 1994), 216.

[16] "This deceitfulness is however only a symptom of the deep depravity, the incurable sickness by which the heart is possessed" (John Peter Lange et al., *A Commentary on the Holy Scriptures: Jeremiah* [Bellingham, Wash.: Logos Bible Software, 2008], 166).

problem, which is the heart.[17] The parent or counselor who rejects God's wisdom regarding a children's behavior likewise rejects God's remedy for that child's heart.

Eliminate the Secular Label

After considering the two presuppositions for behavior analysis, some parents or counselors may indeed embrace God's view of man, but at the same time struggle to eliminate the secular label since it has been so widely used and accepted. However, it is imperative that the label be rejected because it is misleading and damaging.

First of all, the label poorly describes the child's problem, second, it encourages faith in the secular presupposition, and third, it falsely categorizes children as hopeless cases. At best, the ADHD label is used to categorize children by their maladaptive behaviors, and in truth, it is a poor description of their true problem. Though Scripture does not view the ADHD behaviors as medical conditions, it does recognize the human tendency of man to distinguish children and others by their behavior, as even a child is known by what he does (Prov 20:11). This understanding explicates secularists' frequent use of labels and the diagnostic system that classifies people based on their similar conduct. The label of ADHD is one example of man's tendency to look on the outward appearance and to pass judgment on children while failing to discern God's insight into the hearts of man.

---

[17] For better understanding of how all those without Christ are biblical fools and a better understanding of biblical anthropology, see appendix A.

Similarly, Proverbs 14:24 states, "The crown of the wise is their wealth, but the folly of fools brings folly." The observable characteristic of the wise who has God's favor (represented metaphorically by the crown) is wealth (i.e., he is prosperous in all that he does; "successful")[18] or honor,[19] just as the observable characteristic of a fool is his foolish behavior.[20] Kidner sees this verse as reading: "The crown of the wise is their wisdom, but folly is the garland of fools."[21] It is clear from Scripture that behaviors do offer observable insight into the hearts of our children.

Though secularists fail to describe man's heart or his behaviors accurately, they do identify eighteen potentially harmful behaviors that must be addressed. An analysis of these behaviors, considered in the light of God's view, can shed tremendous light on the heart of a child. Whereas God judges a child and his behavior to be moral, either being "pure and right" (Prov 20:11) or being "foolish" (Prov 13:16),[22] secularists judge a child's undesirable behavior as a physical disorder of development and label him or her as abnormal.[23]

---

[18] Kinder, *Proverbs*, 36-37, 110; Waltke, *1-15*, 601-2.

[19] The fool's folly does not allow him to be honored (R. N. Whybray, *Proverbs*, New Century Bible Commentary (Grand Rapids: InterVarsity, 1996), 220).

[20] Waltke, *1-15*, 602.

[21] Kidner, *Proverbs*, 110.

[22] As does Proverbs 20:11, 13:16 shows the connection between one's heart and his behavior. Kidner writes, "Here [Prov 13:16], character (whether one would hide it or not) is shown to be written all over one's conduct" (*Proverbs*, 104); see also, Waltke, *1-15*, 566.

[23] Secularists typically refrain from using the word *bad* to describe behavior as it connotes morality. They rather use *maladaptive*, which means showing poor adaptation or dysfunction.

Since its underlying presupposition and theories dismiss God's wisdom, it is important to eliminate the label of ADHD from use. Furthermore, the label directs attention away from Scripture and man's need of salvation and sanctification while offering false justification for man's foolishness. Some secularists criticize believers for pointing out the reality of all men's sinful nature for which Christ can remedy, yet they themselves are comfortable labelling individuals as abnormal, mentally ill, and declaring that no hope for a cure exists. Secular author and psychiatrist, Dr. Peter Breggin speaks on this matter and the reality that our presuppositional view of man determines how we approach those in need. He writes,

> If people who express seemingly irrational ideas are best understood mechanistically, then these people are broken, disordered, or defective devices. If we take the viewpoint that they are persons, beings, or souls in struggle, then an infinite variety of more subtle possibilities comes to mind for understanding and helping those who seem mad, crazy, or deranged.[24]

When we see man as God sees him and approach these same behaviors from God's wisdom and with his terminology, we will discover very quickly that, unlike secularists who admit they have no solutions, God's Word provides all that is needed for life and godliness. What is more, we will approach all children with truth and love.

Investigate External Influences

Clearly the hearts of children are central to this discussion. Children, however, are more than just spiritual beings—they are also physical in nature. It is important then to explore any valid physical maladies and possible environmental elements that may directly influence a child's behavior. This

---

[24] Peter Breggin, *Toxic Psychiatry*, 25.

inquiry should be conducted as soon as possible. Environment can *influence* a child's behavior but environment cannot *cause* certain behaviors. This distinction changes who/what is responsible for behavior and is therefore significant.

Physical Impairments

The first step in helping a child who exhibits ADHD behaviors is to explore all possible influences present in the child's life and eliminate the possibility of valid physical impairments. For example, though the focus of a child's attention is volitional, valid biological hindrances to giving attention do exist: partial blindness or deafness hinder a child's ability to offer attention as they directly impair the eyes and ears. Similarly, brain damage,[25] ear and sinus infections,[26] autism,[27] allergies,[28] thyroid disease,[29] mental disabilities, and physical injuries can also influence one's ability to give attention. These are valid biological impairments that can influence behavior, yet leading secularists deny that these maladies cause the construct of ADHD.[30] Most of these issues are best

---

[25] Robert Moss, *Why Johnny Can't Concentrate: Coping with Attention Deficit Problems* (New York: Bantam, 1990), 3-4.

[26] Priscilla L. Vail, *Learning Styles: Food for Thought and 130 Practical Tips for Teachers K-4* (Rosemont, N.J.: Modern Learning Press, 1992), 24-25.

[27] Daniel Berger II, *Teaching a Child to Pay Attention: Proverbs 4:20-27* (Taylors, S.C.: Alethia International Publications, 2015).

[28] Julian Stuart Haber, *ADHD: The Great Misdiagnosis* (New York: Taylor Trade, 2003), 72-73.

[29] Hallowell and Ratey, *Driven to Distraction*, 120.

[30] Barkley argues: "No doubt you've encountered claims that factors other than those just discussed cause ADHD. Some of these were originally founded in sound hypotheses but have since been disproven. Others are sheer falsehoods; there is not now and never has been any scientific support for them. As we continue to make conclusive findings about ADHD, let us hope that quackery surrounding the subject will vanish. In the meantime, use what you know about the scientific method to sort fact from fiction" (*TCoA*, 75).

examined by a physician (ideally a believer) who can search for any medical issues and give counsel on psychotropic drugs.

When pediatricians examine a child prior to diagnosing him or her with ADHD, they typically first give the child a physical that evaluates the eyes and ears for injuries or defects — looking for potential influences to behavior that would eliminate ADHD as explaining the child's maladaptive behavior.[31] Many times, however, psychiatrists, therapists, and even parents fail to evaluate other physical problems that can influence choices and lifestyles. Children who show impaired sight, hearing, concentration, and communication in all circumstances in life and not just in uninteresting or undesirable activities should see a medical doctor.

Additionally, Scripture indicates that the physical nature of man affects the spiritual and vice versa — man is psychosomatic in nature (Prov 3:7-8).[32] In Psalm 38:1-22 David prayed to God for spiritual healing. In verse 3 of that passage, he confessed the physical consequences of his sin on his own body: "There is no soundness in my flesh because of your indignation; there is no health in my bones because of my sin. For my iniquities have gone over my head; like a heavy burden, they are too heavy for me. My wounds stink and fester because of my foolishness." Spurgeon says of these verses:

> Mental depression tells upon the bodily frame; it is enough to create and foster every disease, and is in itself the most painful of all diseases. Soul sickness tells upon the entire frame; it weakens the body, and then bodily weakness reacts upon the mind. Neither is

---

[31] Haber, 47-48.

[32] "By turning from his sinful nature one experiences spiritual, psychological, and physical healing (restoration to a former state of wellbeing) … In sum, a right relationship with God leads to a state of complete physical and mental well-being, not simply to the absence of illness and disease" (Waltke, 1-15, 246-47).

there any rest in my bones because of my sin. Deeper still the malady penetrates, till the bones are affected. No soundness and no rest are two sad deficiencies; yet these are both consciously gone from every awakened conscience until Jesus gives relief.[33]

Scripture always views man holistically, connecting spiritual health with physical health and vice versa. Ed Welch notes that "Paul could not imagine a person without a corporeal nature (1 Cor 15). The whole person consists of body and spirit together. Both are essential and neither can function in the material realm in isolation of the other."[34]

Difficult Environments

Physical and emotional trauma can likewise hinder a child's thinking, attention, and behavior. Teachers, administrators, and pastors who desire "to help a child should be willing to look to the conduct of the parents and other potential abusers in the child's environment."[35] Children who are frustrated over their parents' divorce, fighting, or anger may misbehave in school, daydream, and be preoccupied with the poor relationships in their homes.[36] Similarly, abused or neglected children will understandably focus on the pain and confusion that others have caused in their lives.[37] Even while addressing the child's responsibility for his own behavior and value system, anyone who seeks to help such children must guide and love them as well acknowledge that they

---

[33] Charles H. Spurgeon, *Treasury of David*, vol. 2 (New York: Funk and Wagnalls, 1885), 221.

[34] Welch, *Blame it on the Brain*, 39-40.

[35] Peter R. Breggin, *Toxic Psychiatry* (New York: St. Martin's Press, 1991), 274.

[36] Andrew Root, "Fading from the Family Portrait," *Christianity Today*, July/August 2012, 70-73. See also Peter R. Breggin, *Toxic Psychiatry* (New York: St. Martin's Press, 1991), 273.

[37] Haber, 67-68.

may be victims of others' sinful behavior. Therefore all facets of a child's life must be examined in order to administer God's grace effectively and to avoid foolishly causing further emotional damage to the child's heart.

Influential Habits

Though the spiritual direction of the child is the primary concern, counselors and parents must also address habits that can affect a child's thinking, behavior, and relationships. Seemingly small, but habitual poor choices in the areas of diet and sleep, though not sinful patterns, can directly and powerfully influence a child.

Dietary Habits

Although no food in itself causes what secularists claim is ADHD,[38] chemicals, sugars, monosodium glutamate, and caffeine are widely regarded as substances that can negatively influence a child's decisions and behaviors.[39] The body relies on amino acids, iron, zinc, magnesium, and fatty acids to replenish brain cells and promote cell growth within the body.[40] This design makes it imperative that a child have foods that maintain physical health, allow clear thinking, and better enable self-control.

---

[38] WebMD, "ADHD Diets"; available from http://www.webmd.com/add-adhd/guide/adhd-diets?page=2; Internet; accessed 14 August 2012.

[39] Keith Low, "ADHD and Diet: Improving ADHD Symptoms with Diet"; available from http://add.about.com/od/childrenandteens/a/Nutrition.htm; Internet; accessed 14 August 2012.

[40] Vincent J. Monastra, *Parenting Children with ADHD: 10 Lessons that Medicine Cannot Teach* (Washington, D.C.: American Psychological Association, 2005), 76.

Whereas some secularists theorize that malnutrition can cause bad behavior,[41] food in itself does not control man's will unless it contains a controlling substance such as alcohol. Likewise, malnutrition and lack of sleep by themselves never cause sinful behavior, yet they can affect a child's and an adult's abilities to make God-pleasing decisions and walk in holiness.

Sleep Patterns

Similarly, sleep is a major factor in a child's life. It should not be a surprise that parents commonly report that their ADHD children have difficulty sleeping.[42] Right sleep habits are essential for proper physical growth as well as mental, spiritual, and social development.[43] The National Institute of Neurological Disorders has found that sleep deprivation greatly influences human behavior (which, in turn, can influence relationships).

> Sleep appears necessary for our nervous systems to work properly. Too little sleep leaves us drowsy and unable to concentrate the next day. It also leads to impaired memory and physical performance and reduced ability to carry out math calculations. If sleep deprivation continues, hallucinations and mood swings may develop. Some experts believe sleep gives neurons used while we are awake a chance to shut down and repair themselves. Without sleep, neurons may become so depleted in energy or so polluted with byproducts of normal cellular activities that they begin to malfunction. Sleep also

---

[41] Haber, 135-39.

[42] WebMD, "*ADHD and Sleep Disorders*"; available from http://www.webmd.com/add-adhd/guide/adhd-sleep-disorders; Internet; accessed 14 August 2012. Jay Adams states that Proverbs 3:24 speaks directly to why many people cannot sleep: they lack trust in God and instead worry. Those who possess wisdom can rest at night in *sweet sleep* (Jay Adams, *The Christian Counselor's Commentary: Proverbs* [Woodruff, S.C.: Timeless Texts, 1997], 34). See also Tremper Longman III, *Proverbs*, Baker Commentary on the Old Testament Wisdom and Psalms (Grand Rapids: Baker, 2006), 142. Parents with older children must consider and, if necessary, adjust the mindset and activities leading up to bedtime.

[43] Monastra, 75.

may give the brain a chance to exercise important neuronal connections that might otherwise deteriorate from lack of activity.[44]

A child's lack of sleep or poor quality of sleep can influence his thinking, ability to learn,[45] his emotions,[46] and his behaviors.[47] Richard Saul points out that 100 percent of his patients who have problems sleeping also struggle to pay attention, to remain focused, and to have self-control.[48] The Mayo clinic suggests that children from infancy to adulthood require nine to eleven hours of sleep each night, and they recommend an additional three-hour nap for younger children to maintain proper health.[49] Studies show "that people who sleep so little over many nights don't perform as well on complex mental tasks as do people who get closer to seven hours of sleep a night."[50] If research is correct, then an increase in quality sleep should enhance a child's academic performance.

---

[44] National Institute of Neurological Disorders and Strokes, "Brain Basics: Understanding Sleep"; available from http://www.ninds.nih.gov/disorders/brain_basics/understanding_sleep.htm; Internet.

[45] Jennifer Warner, "The Fight for Adequate Sleep . . . in Preschool?"; available from http://www.everydayhealth.com/news/fight-for-adequate-sleep-preschool/?xid=aol_eh-sleep_1_20140224_&aolcat=AJA&icid=maing-grid7%7Cmain5%7Cdl17%7Csec1_lnk3%26pLid%3D449822; Internet.

[46] Higbee, "'Tony' and Bipolar Disorder," 174.

[47] Richard Saul, *ADHD Does Not Exist: The Truth about Attention Deficit and Hyperactivity Disorder* (New York: HarperCollins, 2014), 51-63.

[48] Ibid., 59.

[49] Timothy Morganthaler, "How Many Hours of Sleep Are Enough for Good Health?"; available from http://www.mayoclinic.org/healthy-living/adult-health/expert-answers/how-many-hours-of-sleep-are-enough/faq-20057898; Internet.

[50] Ibid.

Biblically Delineate ADHD Behaviors

After investigating valid physical maladies and possible environmental factors that could be influencing a child's behaviors, counselors and parents should consider each *DSM* behavior that characterizes the child. Though Scripture and secularists may both agree that the behaviors found in the *DSM* are destructive and require attention,[51] they disagree on the moral nature of those behaviors, their nomenclature, their cause, and their remedy. Scripture reveals God's opinion on all the ADHD behaviors, leaving no doubt as to the cause of the behaviors often categorized as ADHD.

Biblically Address ADHD Behaviors

Because of the sobering truth that ADHD behaviors are destructive, counselors must discover which behaviors characterize the child and then address them scripturally. As previously noted, the *DSM* lists specific behaviors within three identified categories that characterize children diagnosed with ADHD: inattention, hyperactivity, and impulsivity.[52]

ADHD- Inattention (ADHD-I)

Though the ADHD label suggests that attention is quantitative and a deficiency can exist,[53] secularists admit that "an actual deficit in attention in

---

[51] *TCoA*, ix.

[52] American Psychiatric Association, *Diagnostic and Statistical Manual of Mental Disorders: DSM-IV-TR* (Washington, D.C.: American Psychiatric Association, 2000), 92-93. Hereafter referred to as *DSM*.

[53] Russell A. Barkley, *ADHD and the Nature of Self-Control* (New York: Guilford, 2005), viii. Hereafter referred to as *NoSC*.

children with ADHD has not been found."[54] Rather than a hypothesis that claims attention is a measurable neurological disposition,[55] Scripture reveals that giving attention is a matter of learned obedience (Prov 1:5 4:1-4, 20; 5:1)[56] and an indicator of one's values (Prov 7:1-4; 8:10-11).[57] Both of these truths are developed further in the book *Teaching a Child to Pay Attention: Proverbs 4:20-27*.[58]

Biblical View of Attention

The Old Testament establishes attention as a child's responsibility: "Hear, O sons, a father's instruction, and be attentive, that you may gain insight"

---

[54] Ibid., 79.

[55] Paul Wender, *ADHD: Attention-Deficit Hyperactivity Disorder in Children, Adolescents, and Adults* (New York: Oxford University Press, 2000), 35-36.

[56] Waltke writes concerning the Hebrew word *hearing*: "[Hearing] signifies to give one's ear to the speaker's words externally and to obey them inwardly" (*1-15*, 177). He goes on to write, "*Learning* (*leqah*; see 4:2) represents the same Hebrew root rendered 'accept' in 1:3 and means getting a grasp on what the teacher wishes to convey'" (179). The biblical concept of hearing (one aspect of attention), then, is not separate from obedience but rather is its beginning.

[57] Kidner sees the logical connection of hearing, valuing, and obedience (*Proverbs*, 75). He views the metaphor of binding the father's words in verse 3 (and also in 3:3) to reflect the child's response of "glorying" in them, "meditating" upon them, and "acting by them" (ibid., 63, 77). Giving attention is not merely the intake of information but treasuring it, repeating it, and then acting upon it. Even parental commands that may lack value to the child are based upon a value system of the father/son relationship. In other words, a child who values his relationship with his parents (and with God) will value his parent's instructions. A child should treasure his godly parent's wisdom and instructions (based on and founded on divine commands) above even rare treasure (Prov 8:10) (Ibid., 77). Waltke, like Kidner, sees the father in 8:10 desiring his son to listen to him and make his wisdom the affection of his heart (*1-15*, 399). Proverbs implies that the value the son should find in the commands comes from the value he finds in the relationship with his authority—the father's authority comes from God. Longman writes, "At the very least, we can say that the words the father is urging on the son come with a great deal of authority" (119). Thus the commands of God are written as the father's own (ibid., 119-20). Ultimately, the value in parental commands and instructions comes from the authority and creative order of God.

[58] Daniel Berger II, *Teaching a Child to Pay Attention: Proverbs 4:20-27* (Taylors, S.C.: Alethia International Publications, 2015).

(Prov 4:1).[59] These injunctions reveal that attention is volitional and thus a spiritual matter that requires both the child's obedience to parental instructions and his learning of valuable wisdom. Scripture assumes that he who has an ear to hear, according to God's natural design (Prov 20:12),[60] should willfully offer his attention to his authority (Matt 11:15).[61] With the exception of valid physical hindrances that impair hearing or sight, God has made children fully capable of giving attention and holds them responsible to do so. Waltke emphasizes that the "responsibility to respond to instruction lies squarely on the child's shoulders; he must listen to it (Prov 1:8), accept it (1:3; 19:20; 23:23), love it (12:1), prize it more highly than money (4:7; 23:23), and not let go of it (4:13)." Both maturity and responsibility are developmental, and believing parents must start teaching their children at an early age the importance of paying attention and valuing their instructions.[62] This teaching, of course, must be age-appropriate and must

---

[59] The father's imperative command to his son to pay attention is repeated ten times in chapters 1-9 of Proverbs (Whybray, 23-30).

[60] Longman suggests that this proverb not only shows Yahweh's goodness in providing man with hearing and seeing, but he implies that the proverb gives deeper insight by directing the reader's attention toward grace. Physically and spiritually "there is no seeing or hearing apart from his good gift" (380). Similarly, Waltke sees the same usages throughout Proverbs. He writes that "hearing (or listen) almost always connotes 'to listen and obey,'" but he points out that the eye is used to refer to "moral discernment" and not just physical sight (15-31, 140-41). Worthy of noting is the phrase "has made" which "in the Old Testament indicates God's creative achievements" (ibid., 141). Kidner also sees this verse as pointing to Ephesians 2:8-10 and salvation "by grace alone" (*Proverbs*, 138). God designed the eyes and ears with the specific purposes of education and relationship.

[61] "A proverbial expression to evoke attention" (John Peter Lange and Philip Schaff. *A Commentary on the Holy Scriptures: Matthew* [Bellingham, Wash.: Logos Bible Software, 2008], 206).

[62] Waltke writes that within the historical context of Proverbs, a father began "stern teaching" after the child had been weaned/after three years of age (1-15, 277). Since each child is different, parents should assess their children individually and approach their education according to how God has created them (15-31, 205).

include training children to use their eyes and ears in a way that pleases God. Additionally, this education must start at an early age.

Not only does Scripture teach that children are responsible to give attention correctly, but it also shows that the object of this attention reveals the heart's affections (Prov 8:10-21)[63] and thus his life's direction (8:32-36). Scripture describes attention as one's willful act of using the senses to receive information that is deemed important (Prov 2:1-6).[64] In other words, people express their value system/reveal their pursuits through the focus of their eyes, ears, and hearts (Prov 4:20-27). Man's depraved and deceived heart, however, naturally esteems his own wisdom above God's and thus embraces a self-centered lifestyle (Prov 3:7-8), focuses his attention on self (pride), and focuses on things that lack actual value (worldliness).[65] Man's tendency to disregard the instructions of his

---

[63] Waltke writes: "*Those who love me* [wisdom] implicitly states the heart's affections for receiving her communicable virtues" (*1-15*, 404). In discussing Proverbs 8:35, Waltke connects the mature sons paying close attention (35) with his doing the will and pleasure of another. As he listens to wisdom and receives it ("involving one's desire"), he in turn receives God's pleasure — "acceptance, approval, delight of another" (Waltke, *1-15*, 425). To whom or what one gives attention not only reveals that person's desires but determines if the anticipated hearer is approved and an object of delight to the teacher. This is true not only on a vertical plane with God and man, but also in human relationships (e.g., father/son). The child who does not listen to (delight in) his father and mother will bring them shame and sorrow compared to the joy and delight of the child who learns to listen "(Prov 10:1; 17:21)" (Waltke, *15-31*, 60). Likewise, the child who does not obey his parents in everything ultimately displeases the Lord (Col 3:20). The child who is disciplined (taught to receive divine wisdom), however, will bring his parents delight and his behaviors will come from a heart that pleases God.

[64] One example is the hearing ear, which Waltke notes, without its use, memorization and ultimately heart changes will not occur in the child's life (ibid., 220-21). He also states, "According to [Prov] 2:2 the ear (4:20) is the key to the heart (v. 23)" (ibid., 295). Unfortunately, the naturally foolish heart chooses to use the senses to live according to his own wisdom instead of pleasing God (Waltke, *15-31*, 140-41). Kidner also points out that the process of education (he speaks of moral education) must involve both the child's exploring teachings and instructions as well as treasuring them (*Proverbs*, 61).

[65] "Worldliness is one of the greatest dangers that beset the human soul. It is no wonder that we find our Lord speaking strongly about it: it is an insidious, specious, plausible enemy; it

authority is the result of his naturally proud heart and misplaced desires. This tendency explains why children choose to esteem their own desires and thoughts as more valuable than those of their parents, teachers, and friends, and consequently, direct their attention accordingly (Prov 18:1-2).[66] Proverbs 18:1 also teaches that those who shun valuable relationships do so unwisely in order to pursue their own desires; it also describes "those who are internally focused on their own desires, but such a focus would naturally separate them from the community."[67]

Whereas the Old Testament provides man with the foundation for understanding God's design and his intended focus for man's attention, the New Testament assumes God's design and thus commands children to obey their parents (Eph 6:1) and to honor or esteem them as valuable (Eph 6:2).[68] Both

---

seems so innocent *to pay close attention to our business* [emphasis added]! It seems so harmless to seek our happiness in this world, so long as we keep clear of open sins! Yet here is a rock on which many are shipwrecked for all eternity. They 'store up ... treasures on earth,' and forget to 'store up ... treasures in heaven' (verses 19–20). May we all remember this! Where are our hearts? What do we love best? Are our chief affections on things on earth, or things in heaven? Life or death depends on the answer we can give to these questions. If our treasure is earthly, our hearts will be earthly too. 'For where your treasure is, there your heart will be also' (verse 21)" (J. C. Ryle, *Matthew*, Crossway Classic Commentaries, ed. Alister McGrath and J. I. Packer [Wheaton: Crossway, 1993], 43).

[66] Murphy also recognizes the logical conclusion—the individual who seeks his own desires, is antisocial, and who blurts out his own opinions is a "fool (Prov 12:16, 23; 13:16)" (134–35). Similarly, Adams writes, "[The child] is so wrapped up in himself and what he is doing that, for all he cares, the world can go hang... here is the child who doesn't need his parents" (Jay Adams, *The Christian Counselor's Commentary: Proverbs* [Woodruff, S.C.: Timeless Texts, 1997], 143). Hereafter referred to as *CCC Proverbs*.

[67] Longman, 354.

[68] *Honor* (τιμάω) usually means to value, to set a price on, or to greatly esteem. John MacArthur writes: "The right *attitude* behind the right act of obedience is honor (τιμάω), which means to value highly, to hold in the highest regard and respect" (John MacArthur, *Ephesians*, MacArthur New Testament Commentary [Chicago: Moody, 1986], 312). "Honor refers to the public acknowledgment of a person's worth, granted on the basis of how fully that individual embodies qualities and behaviors valued by the group" (Stanley E. Porter and Craig A. Evans, *Dictionary of New Testament Background: A Compendium of Contemporary Biblical Scholarship* [Downers Grove: InterVarsity, 2000], 518). "While honor is an internal attitude of respect,

obedience and honor are volitional, and they reflect and depend upon a child's right focus. Children who value divine wisdom (Prov 4:7)[69] will also highly esteem their parents' instructions, warnings, rules, values, and corrections, and this right value system will lead them to obedient behavior[70] set on pleasing the Lord (Col 3:20). If a child chooses to esteem something more highly than God (idolatry), then his attention will be misdirected, and his behaviors will be unrestrained and disobedient (Prov 29:18).[71]

---

courtesy, and reverence, it should be accompanied by appropriate attention or even obedience. Honor without such action is incomplete; it is lip service (Isa. 29:13). God the Father, for example, is honored when people do the things that please him (1 Cor. 6:20). Parents are honored through the obedience of their children" (Sam Hamstra Jr., "Honor," *Evangelical Dictionary of Biblical Theology*, ed. Walter A. Elwell [Grand Rapids: Baker, 1996]). In summary, honor is a two-directional mindset that (1) fixes one's attention and (2) produces obedience that pleases the Lord. Right attention (eyes and ears) produces a right mindset which in turn produces right motives, desires, and directions. A child's obedience without a right heart change falls short of pleasing the Lord (it is not done "in the Lord" [Eph 6:1]).

[69] Clarke says of this verse, "Let [wisdom] be thy chief property" (*Proverbs*, Proverbs 4:7).

[70] Ephesians 6:1 states that a child's obedience is *right*, which is a judicial term indicating that the child's behaviors should be just. Solomon also stated in Proverbs 1:2-4 that the result of parental teaching and application of wisdom leads children to just and equitable behavior. Waltke emphasizes that the child's wise behaviors are "*right* [or 'righteous,' *sedq*], and *just* [or 'justice,' *mispat*], and *fair* [or 'upright,' *mesarim*]" (Waltke, 1-15, 177). Similarly, Jamieson, Fausset, and Brown point out that the child's obedience is demanded by *both natural law* and *revealed law*. Robert Jamieson, A. R. Fausset, and David Brown, *A Commentary Critical and Explanatory on the Whole Bible* [Oak Harbor, Wash.: Logos Research Systems, Inc., 1997], Eph 6:2). Proverbs teaches that a child becomes just, righteous, and equitable through "discipline of wisdom" (Proverbs 1:3). Cohen writes, "The reader [of Proverbs] will be taught how to acquire the discipline which will enable him to perceive the line of conduct that is just and right" (2).

[71] "Instruction [based on divine wisdom] is now said to effect *prudent behavior* (*haskel*, i.e., wise behavior," "good sense"; see p. 94) as the first of its benefits. This changed behavior is not maladaptive or destructive to the community, but "that which serves and heals the community." One's true attention both reveals the heart and ultimately determines one's behaviors (Waltke, 1-5, 177); see also Longman, 410-11. Proverbs 29:18 is discussed further in chapter 4.

Alleged *ADHD-I*, then, is not a biological deficiency in one's ability to give attention, but rather a child's natural inclination to value his own desires over the instructions of his authority and to choose the path which he perceives is most convenient. This natural tendency reveals an immature and foolish child who believes that his own opinions, desires, and perceptions of life are more valuable than pleasing God and listening to his authorities' instructions.

Biblical View of the *DSM* Inattentive Behaviors

Similarly, children diagnosed with ADHD-*I* will exhibit behaviors found under the category of inattention. Secularists list the child's behaviors as: (1) "often does not *give close attention* [emphasis added] to details or makes careless mistakes in schoolwork, work, or other activities," (2) "often has trouble keeping attention on task or play activities," (3) and "often *does not seem to listen* [emphasis added] when spoken to directly."[72] As previously stated, the object of a person's attention reflects desires and values. If children choose to not listen to their parents, they reveal their desire to get their own way and to honor themselves above others. These behaviors are not abnormal, but normal childish actions that require parents to teach and supervise their children from the earliest of years.

Secularists also describe the child diagnosed with ADHD as one who "often does not follow through on instructions and fails to finish schoolwork, chores, or duties in the workplace (not due to oppositional behavior or failure to understand instructions)."[73] Scripture addresses this behavior in numerous

---

[72] *DSM*, 92.

[73] Ibid., 92.

passages such as Proverbs 6:6-11, which reveals that the natural heart of the child is slothful, and if left alone, the child will grow to become a sluggard. The first section of this passage (6-8) directs the learner to obtain wisdom from the ant, which, without supervision, takes initiative and shows responsibility to complete its tasks. The second portion warns the child that laziness is counterproductive to success and that he is accountable (9-11). Both sections, as well as Proverbs 10:4-5, judge the individual capable of understanding who neglects his responsibilities, who lacks diligence, and who does not complete tasks to be slothful. Kidner notes in his commentary on Proverbs four common characteristics of the sluggard which mirror closely some of the behaviors characteristic of children diagnosed with ADHD: (1) he will not start tasks on his own initiative, (2) he will not finish things without supervision, (3) he will not take responsibility for his failures, and (4) "consequently he is restless with unsatisfied desire."[74]

As described in the *DSM* definition of ADHD, children who are slothful need constant supervision to complete tasks since they lack the diligence and self-motivation exemplified by the ant: "Signs of the disorder [ADHD] may be minimal or absent when the person is under close supervision."[75] This explanation does not describe abnormal activity in children but describes normalcy, since by nature, all children need supervision to accomplish tasks until parents can cultivate maturity, right motivation, self-control, and right values in their lives. In his discussion on the sluggard, Kidner also concludes that the

---

[74] Kidner, *Proverbs*, 43.

[75] *DSM*, 86-87.

sluggard is not abnormal. He writes, "[The wise man] knows that the sluggard is no freak, but, as often as not, an ordinary man who has made too many excuses, too many refusals and too many postponements. It has all been as imperceptible, and as pleasant, as falling asleep."[76] The young child who is given excuses for his self-centered nature and his disobedience and who is not taught right pursuits and motives is on his way to forming a lifestyle of slothfulness (becoming a sluggard).[77] Though Proverbs views a sluggard as an older individual, being slothful is a common condition of fallen man and can be seen even in younger children.[78]

Not only is the foolish heart naturally slothful, but it is likewise disobedient. Assuming that the child understands instructions and that the instructions are age-appropriate, the child's failure to follow instructions can reveal a heart that does not value his authorities' wisdom and that lacks the desire to please the Lord (Col 3:20). The child may desire better academic success, better relationships, parental praise, and better experiential outcomes in

---

[76] Kidner, *Proverbs*, 43.

[77] He is a sluggard because of his depraved "habits" which most often begin in his childhood (ibid., 42-43).

[78] Kidner shows that the simple fool, like the sluggard, chases after vanities (12:11) and is characterized by "lazy thoughtlessness" (ibid., 39). In his commentary on Proverbs 12:11, Longman states, "Perhaps it may be said that those who lack substance (heart) pursue that which lacks substance ('emptiness')" (274). Waltke sees the same comparison and explains, "A foolish son shows his moral degeneracy by his laziness (cf. Eccl 10:18). In 6:6 the sluggard is admonished to 'become wise,' the antithesis of being a fool; in 24:30 the sluggard is said to 'lack sense'; and in 26:12-16 the sluggard is said to be more despicable than a fool. In other words, this partial subunit escalates his being a fool (19:13) to his being a sluggard (19:15)" (Waltke, *15-31*, 109).

life, but his excuses and lack of parental honor and obedience will result in unrealized desires, incomplete work, and lack of success (Prov 13:4; 20:4).[79]

The *DSM* also describes the ADHD child as one who "often avoids, dislikes, or *doesn't want to do things* [emphasis added] that take a lot of mental effort for a long period of time."[80] Proverbs 28:19 describes this unwise characteristic: "Whoever works his land will have plenty of bread, but he who follows worthless pursuits will have plenty of poverty."[81] By nature, children (and adults) want the easiest way, and, in pursuit of amusement and immediate self-indulgence, they often avoid what requires sustained effort. Even secular counselors recognize that children base their immature value systems on what best pleases them now, rather than on future reward.[82] This tendency is evidenced in children labelled as ADHD who lack maturity and desire to complete their homework, yet they are able to sustain uninterrupted mental effort as they play video games for hours. In contrast, Proverbs 17:24 describes the discerning man as one who diligently sets his attention on wisdom instead of vanity. That Proverbs 17:24 mentions the eyes of the fool is important because it

---

[79] "Proverbs is intolerant of lazy people; they are considered the epitome of folly" (Longman, 561-62).

[80] *DSM*, 92.

[81] This proverb contrasts the diligent worker who will have his needs met, with the foolish who pursues vanity and will always be in need. Kidner recognizes the symmetry of 28:19 and 12:11: the sluggard does not lack energy, but discrimination in what is worth following (*Proverbs*, 96-97). Some translations see the one lacking discernment as pursuing vain people, but as Steveson notes, "vain things" is more likely in mind (398).

[82] *NoSC*, 58-63.

indicates that the object of the fool's attention is vanity rather than wisdom.[83] The child who avoids responsibilities in pursuit of pleasure is living according to the foolishness that is bound in his natural heart.

Two other behavioral patterns of inattention are listed in the *DSM:* a child "often loses things needed for tasks and activities" and "often is forgetful in daily activities."[84] Although Scripture does not identify these common behaviors as sin, these behaviors do describe the fallen condition of every man since people tend to forget and lose things of value. Newheiser notes, "We remember what is most important to us. The son who often forgets his homework never forgets his soccer game."[85] Like giving attention, forgetfulness and losing possessions are matters of a child's value system, maturity, and focus in life.

People are forgetful when they fail to see enough value in prioritizing and retaining information. Proverbs 4:4-10 conveys the truth that remembering requires sustained effort, willful obedience (4-5),[86] and a discovery of value (6-10). Similarly, Waltke writes concerning Proverbs 2:2,

---

[83] Waltke notes, "The imprecision suggests that the eyes of the wise focus on wisdom, which in turn serves him well, but the fool's focus flits from one godless, unattainable thing to another that does not profit him" *(15-31, 62).*

[84] *DSM*, 92.

[85] Jim Newheiser, *Opening Up Proverbs* (Leominster, England: Day One Publications, 2008), 59.

[86] To remember or not forget something assumes that it has been first acquired. The son was commanded to "acquire Wisdom" and to "not forget nor turn away" from wisdom (Longman, 149-50). Waltke also notes the two metaphors that are used in the father's (grandfather's) commands: (1) the metaphor of economy—the son was to use all his resources to buy wisdom (2) the metaphor of love or marriage—the son was to value and be intimate with wisdom, forsaking all others. This would not be a one-time decision, but a lifelong dedication that would cost him everything *(1-15, 279).* Longman also states of Proverbs 3:1: "Not to forget is to remember; and to remember something in the OT means more than mere cognitive retention. To remember, or not to forget, means to obey. That the son's obedience is to be more than a superficial matter is specified in the second colon, where it is his heart, standing for his core

"Accept" is escalated to store up (treasure), which means, with the accusative of thing, to hide or conceal for a definite purpose (cf. Ps 119:11). That notion entails that one treasures that which he stores (see 2:4; 10:14; Job 15:20; 21:19; Hos 13:12). The metaphor signifies to memorize with religious affection Solomon's "sound bites" in order to have them ready when the occasion demands them (cf. 5:2; 7:1; 22:18; cf. Job 23:12; Ps 119:11).[87]

The principles that apply to remembering the most important parental instructions (divine wisdom) also apply to temporal instructions. For example, as children esteem amusing activities more desirable than responsibilities or obedience, they can lose focus and forget to complete tasks or forget important possessions. Though the *DSM* portrays *ADHD-I* children as "often forgetful in daily activities," these activities are selective, since most children diagnosed with ADHD remember daily activities such as how to operate their MP3 players, their favorite video game's logins and passwords, and lines from their favorite movies. Remembering and paying attention are closely linked since remembering is the willful, ongoing act of committing one's attention to something of value.[88]

Wise children diligently work to remember and treasure important possessions just as God expects his children to remember his covenants, his commands, his character, and his works. Though forgetfulness may not be a sin of commission, it can reveal one's value system and a child's immaturity.

---

personality, [sic] that is to protect the commands. Again, protection means to observe the commands that are to be deeply embedded in the son" (131).

[87] "Its method is not one of free speculation, but of treasuring and exploring received teachings so as to penetrate to their principles" (Kidner, *Proverbs*, 61). See also Waltke, 1-15, 220.

[88] Waltke's view is consistent with that of the philosopher of science Michael Polanyi who said, "True knowledge flows from personal commitment to a set of particulars, as tools or clues, to shape a skillful achievement, not from detached observation of them." Remembering is the act of committing one's mind to a set of particulars (ibid., 219).

Additionally, God's plan of evangelism through the work of the Holy Spirit is also accomplished through communication that requires an instructor and a hearer (Rom 10:14-18). In like manner, sanctification requires that the hearer obey God's Word (as he is able to understand) rather than forget it (Jas 1:22-27).[89] Attention is foundational to the gospel, discipleship, parenting, education, counseling, and every important human relationship. Therefore, attempts to redefine attention apart from God's design are deceptive and destructive, and they attack God's plan for social, familial, and ecclesiastical structure and growth.

Scripture also deems all of the other *DSM* criteria under inattention to be behavior that is common to man rather than abnormal. The Bible describes many of these behaviors to be products of a heart that is naturally foolish, slothful, unwise, and lacking self-control. These are the reliable judgments of God which describe the child who volitionally or ignorantly chooses to value himself over God's will and whom secularists label as having *ADHD-I*. It is important to understand that the child is not abnormal, but naturally depraved and in need of maturity and God's wisdom.

ADHD – Hyperactivity (Part of ADHD-HI)

And what about hyperactivity? Scripture does not regard hyperactivity to be sin against God, yet it does declare uncontrolled thoughts, emotions, and

---

[89] Derek Kidner comments on the repetition of the father's call to his son to give him his attention as deliberate and important since it reveals that "a major part of godliness lies in dogged attentiveness to familiar truths" (*Proverbs*, 68). "'Hearing and doing' God's will, with the corollary that believers should not be quick to follow their own desires and designs, is a common theme in the Wisdom literature: see Prov 10:9; 13:3; 15:1; 29:20; Eccl 7:9; 9:18" (Ralph P. Martin, *James*, vol. 48 of Word Biblical Commentary [Dallas: Word, 1998], 47).

behaviors to be unwise and destructive. High energy and continuous movement are often positive qualities in God's design for specific people when controlled, and believers should not consider these traits counterproductive or sinful. Yet, the person who lacks control over his spirit is compared to a city without walls that is open to destruction (Prov 25:28).[90]

Biblical View of Hyperactivity

The Bible does not view high energy (traditional meaning of hyperactivity) as a negative character quality, and some secular writers agree. For example, Hallowell and Ratey argue, "Although ADD can generate a host of problems, there are also advantages to having it . . . such as high energy, intuitiveness, creativity, and enthusiasm, and they are completely overlooked by the 'disorder' model."[91] Society often considers children with high energy to be problematic, but in reality, the child's high energy is part of God's design and may be necessary for future service or life-calling. Pastors and teachers are often highly energetic, enthusiastic, and intuitive people who positively influence students and others in their lives. These personality traits please God when they are directed and Spirit-controlled for God's purpose and glory. Policemen, firefighters, educators, counselors, politicians, doctors, counselors, health

---

[90] Waltke writes that lack of self-control characterizes the fool and is illustrated in Proverbs 25:28 by the absence of walls (*15-31*, 344). Waltke explains the depth of this metaphor in describing three parallels to the defenseless city without walls and the fool: (1) Without self-control, sin will master him. He states: "Freud may have first articulated psychologically that we are not masters in our house, ruled as we are by unruly passions, but he is not the first to discern it. Proverbs knows the power of sin that drives one to death" (344). (2) The fool is open to society's retributions for his unrestrained folly that have hurt them. (3) Last, he is an easy target for the wicked who wish to destroy him (Waltke, *15-31*, 344).

[91] Hallowell and Ratey, *Driven to Distraction*, xi.

70

technicians, artists, athletes, and salesmen are just some of the career choices in which high-energy individuals often excel.[92]

In retrospect, secularists have diagnosed some of the most successful and high-energy athletes to have had ADHD,[93] and they consider many well-known world leaders and prominent figures throughout history to have also had ADHD.[94] The vast majority of these individuals were successful in their respected areas without the use of medications or the stigma of the ADHD label.

Biblical View of the *DSM* Hyperactivity Behaviors

Though Scripture does not specifically address the traditional understanding of hyperactivity ("highly energetic or excessively active"),[95] it does address the *DSM's* definition which combines a child's expected obedience with his lack of self-control. To understand this subtype, it is helpful to divide the six criteria under hyperactivity into two separate groups. The first three *DSM* behaviors under hyperactivity pertain to a child's behavior in relation to the expectations and rules of his authority, and the second group describes his lack of self-control.

The first three criteria in the *DSM* list are "often gets up from his seat *when remaining in seat is expected* [emphasis added]," "often fidgets with hands or feet or squirms in seat *when sitting still is expected* [emphasis added]," and "often

---

[92] Hallowell and Ratey, *Delivered from Distraction*, 4.

[93] "Famous People with ADHD;" available from http://adhdandmore.blogspot.com /2009/ 01/famous-people-with-adhd.html; Internet.

[94] Ibid.

[95] S.v. "hyperactivity"; available from http://www.merriam-webster.com/dictionary /hyperactivity; Internet.

excessively runs about or climbs *when and where it is not appropriate* [emphasis added]."[96] Though secularists classify these three criteria as hyperactivity, they, in truth, describe a child's disobedience toward authority. Secularists suggest that this disobedience should be excused since, they theorize, ADHD children are physically and mentally incapable of obedience.[97] In their view, "ADHD impairs the human will and volition,"[98] so authorities should not expect the child to obey.

If, however, authorities are responsible and establish clear and appropriate boundaries, and if the child understands the expectations, then Scripture judges the child who violates these rules to be disobedient and not merely hyperactive as the *DSM* suggests.[99] Scripture pronounces these behaviors as injustice to both God and the parent (Eph 6:1)[100] to the extent that in the Old

---

[96] *DSM*, 92.

[97] *NoSC*, 315.

[98] Ibid.

[99] Parents should consider the possibility that they may not be clearly communicating their expectations to their children, as Joseph and Mary illustrate. Christ was not in sin for remaining in Jerusalem since he was always obedient to God (Lk 2:49) and always submissive to his parents (2:51). "Joseph and Mary *were astonished.* Clearly they had expected nothing like this. There is reproach in Mary's question, *Son, why have you treated us so?* and in her reference to their anxious search. For Jesus it was a matter of surprise that there should have been any difficulty. The natural place for him to be was *in my Father's house*" (Leon Morris, *Luke: An Introduction and Commentary*, vol. 3 of Tyndale New Testament Commentaries [Downers Grove: InterVarsity, 1988], 108–9). Clear parental instruction is essential for children to understand and to be obedient to their parents' expectations.

[100] Foulkes notes: "Even children, in their simple way, can know what it means to love in the Lord, and to obey for his sake. The reason given for obedience is striking in its austerity: for this is right. Perhaps his thought is that it is accepted as proper in every society; it is right by the Old Testament law; it is in accordance with the example of Christ himself (Luke 2:51). Or it may be that the form of his expression was intended to carry the reminder that in some things children must accept and follow before they can see all the reasons" (*Ephesians*, 168). Regarding Ephesians 6:1, Hodge writes, "**Children, obey your parents.** The nature of character of this

Testament excessive disobedience (rejection of parental authority or rebellion) was punishable by death (Deut 21:18).[101] Though God's grace is longsuffering toward rebellious children, rebellion remains a serious sin against God and man (Rom 1:30-32).

Whereas the first three behaviors under hyperactivity are disobedience, the second three *DSM* behaviors are matters of self-control and immaturity. They describe a child who "often has trouble playing or doing leisure activities quietly,"[102] "often talks excessively," and "is often 'on the go' or acts as if 'driven by a motor.'"[103] Two of the behaviors pertain to a child who lacks control of his mouth (see Prov 21:23) and whose speech is loud and excessive. Scripture consistently contrasts the foolish individual who is loud (Prov 9:13) with the wise

---

obedience is expressed by the words **in the Lord.** It should be religious, arising out of the conviction that such obedience is the will of **the Lord.** This makes it a higher service than if done out of fear or from mere natural affection. Such a motive makes sure that the obedience is prompt, kindly, and universal. That **Lord** here refers to Christ is clear from the whole context. In Ephesians 5:21 we have the general exhortation under which this special direction to children is included, and the obedience there required is **out of reverence for Christ.** In the following verses also **Lord** constantly has this reference and therefore must have it here. The ground of the obligation to filial obedience is expressed in the words, **for this is right.** It is not because of the personal character of the parent, nor because of his kindness, nor on the ground of expediency but because it is **right**—an obligation arising out of the nature of the relationship between parents and children, and which must exist wherever the relationship itself exists" (Charles Hodge, *Ephesians,* vol. 7 of Crossway Classic Commentaries, ed. Alister McGrath and J. I. Packer [Wheaton: Crossway, 1994], 202).

[101] "We may have here another example of a penalty stated in an extreme form in order to underline the serious nature of the crime. . . . While no example of the carrying out of this sentence occurs in the pages of the Old Testament, the prescriptions underlined the seriousness of the offence. . . . In Jesus' view such an attitude was a breach of the commandment 'Honor your father and your mother' and called forth the judgment, 'He who speaks evil of father or mother, let him surely die'" (J. A. Thompson, *Deuteronomy: An Introduction and Commentary,* vol. 5 of Tyndale Old Testament Commentaries, ed. Donald J. Wiseman [Downers Grove: InterVarsity, 1974], 253).

[102] *DSM,* 92.

[103] Ibid.

individual who is quiet, controlled, and pleasing to God and man. Kidner points out that "the sparing use of words is commended as a mark of a cool spirit', which denotes 'a man of understanding.'"[104] The Bible — especially in the wisdom literature — consistently contrasts a foolish man who lacks control of his tongue with a wise man who strives with the Spirit's help to control his words.[105]

Not only does Scripture address behaviors of the mouth which proceed from the heart, it also addresses the last criterion under hyperactivity, calling it hastiness, which leads to eventual poverty and deeper sin (Prov 19:2).[106] The secularists' description of the child "driven by a motor" does not merely mean high energy, but also a child who has "a tendency not to plan ahead" and is, instead, hasty.[107] Scripture declares hastiness to be characteristic of an immature individual who lacks right focus in life and subsequently lacks plans to achieve success (Prov 21:5).[108] Waltke writes, "The hasty act without moral reflection to avoid the hard discipline of diligence. We should assume that the diligent creatively plan within the framework of God's revealed will and by nature act

---

[104] Kidner also gives three reasons why a controlled tongue is a wise choice: (1) "it allows time for a fair hearing (18:13; verse 17)" (2) "it allows tempers to cool (15:1)" (3) "its influence is potent: 'a soft tongue breaketh the bone' (25:15)" (*Proverbs*, 48).

[105] Moo comments on James 1:19. "The importance of controlling one's speech is a popular theme in wisdom literature (cf. Prov 10:19; 15:1; 17:27-28). . . . Significantly, looseness in speech is often linked with unrestrained anger. According to Proverbs 17:27, 'He who restrains his words has knowledge, and he who has a cool spirit is a man of understanding'" (Douglas J. Moo, *James: An Introduction and Commentary*, vol. 16 of Tyndale New Testament Commentaries Downers Grove: InterVarsity, 1985), 82).

[106] "A person who 'hasteth with his feet' is one who acts without knowing his goal. He hurries into mindless activity with no clear end in mind" (Steveson, 253).

[107] Wender, *ADHD*, 27.

[108] Whereas the lazy lack motivation (right desires) to do what is right, the hasty lack discernment (right thoughts) (Waltke, *15-31*, 172).

accordingly."[109] The child who is hasty naturally goes through life motivated by his wrong desires and behaves accordingly, which is why Kidner recognizes "restlessness" to stem from "unsatisfied desires."[110] This understanding defines most immature children.

Though Scripture pronounces the *DSM* behaviors under hyperactivity to be foolishness and disobedience, high energy, enthusiasm, and intuitiveness are not sinful, undesirable, or abnormal personality traits. Barkley admits, "It is commonplace for children, especially young preschool children, to be active, energetic, and exuberant and to flit from one activity to another as they explore their environment and its novelties."[111] You must be careful to separate your child's normal hyperactivity from willful rebellion.

The *DSM* characteristics of hyperactivity reveal the child's heart to be disobedient, uncontrolled, and indicative of the problematic direction of his life's course. These behaviors are issues of obedience, Spirit-filled self-control, and maturity which believing parents are responsible to exemplify and to cultivate in their children's hearts through the work of the Holy Spirit.

ADHD – Impulsivity (Part of ADHD-HI)

Just as secular psychologists misnamed the second group of *DSM* criteria *hyperactivity*, they also misuse *impulsivity* to describe the third group of criteria.

---

[109] Waltke, *15-31*, 172; although the verse refers to an older child (or adult) being hasty to become rich, the problem of hastiness is a problem of the natural heart even seen in younger children. The idea behind hastiness is that one trusts in his own way in order to get what he wants, and this individual contrasts the one who trusts in the Lord and is diligent in his work while he waits patiently for God's will to be accomplished.

[110] *Proverbs*, 43.

[111] *NoSC*, 1.

All three criteria under *impulsivity* reveal a heart that is naturally consumed with getting one's own way over loving others.

The Biblical View of Impulsivity

Collectively, the *DSM* behaviors depicted as *impulsivity*, in actuality, describe self-centeredness rather than mere impulsivity. These behaviors reflect the natural heart of man which esteems himself as more important than others. Philippians 2:3-5 reflects this truth: "Do nothing from selfish ambition or conceit, but in humility count others more significant than yourselves. Let each of you look not only on his own interests, but also to the interests of others. Have this mind among yourselves, which is yours in Christ Jesus."[112] The *DSM* criteria for impulsivity (which should be labelled as self-centeredness) expose a child's need for the Word of God to renew him with the mind of Christ and to instill in him a loving value system that esteems God and others as more important than himself (Matt 22:36-40).

The Biblical View of the *DSM* Impulsivity Behaviors

The three criteria which comprise the impulsivity grouping in the *DSM* reveal a child's naturally self-centered heart: "often blurts out answers before questions have been finished," "often interrupts or intrudes on others (e.g., butts into conversations or games)," and "often has trouble waiting one's turn."[113]

---

[112] MacArthur states that selfish ambitions (personal goals) are the roots of all sin and an exaggerated self-view (personal glorification) is the root of relational problems. In essence, this defines someone who is a proverbial fool. Here Christ (true wisdom) is the antithesis of the fool, and Christians are to renew their mind in this wisdom (Christ). (John F. MacArthur Jr., *Philippians*, MacArthur New Testament Commentary [Chicago: Moody, 2001], 110–11).

[113] *DSM*, 92.

76

As with hyperactivity, two of the criteria under impulsivity relate to the child's control over his mouth, and older individuals who behave as such are considered by Scripture to be foolish and shameful (Prov 29:20).[114] Proverbs 18:13 conveys this truth: "If one gives an answer before he hears, it is folly and shame." Scripture also considers an individual's frequent interruptions and lack of control of his mouth to be evidence of his self-focus and natural foolishness. Waltke states it as such: "This introductory proverb typically pertains to being teachable. Its subject is implicitly the fool who, before the wise has finished speaking, boorishly interrupts him to spout his own opinion (see 18:2)."[115] Proverbs 17:28 also states, "Even a fool who keeps silent is considered wise; when he closes his lips, he is deemed intelligent."[116] The fool's uncontrolled desire to make his opinion known and his inability to control his emotions reveal his heart.

Because of their hasty words, angry reactions, and self-centeredness, children diagnosed with ADHD often lack good friends.[117] In contrast to man's naturally selfish heart, patience and self-control describe the mature believer (Ti 2:2).[118] Children who behave according to the *DSM*'s criteria for impulsivity

---

[114] This is speech that is not considered before it is delivered (Waltke, *15-31*, 447-48).

[115] Waltke, *15-31*, 79.

[116] "Using humor in the first colon, the sages suggest that the best chance a fool has for being thought intelligent is to avoid speaking" (Longman, 351).

[117] Wender, *ADHD*, 26.

[118] "The first practical outworking of such sound doctrine will be an insistence that behaviour [sic] should tally with belief" (Donald Guthrie, *Pastoral Epistles: An Introduction and Commentary*, vol. 14 of Tyndale New Testament Commentaries [Downers Grove: InterVarsity, 1990], 213).

live from a natural heart that esteems itself better than it should, a heart that

needs to be renewed with the mind of Christ (Rom 12:1-3; Phil 2:3-10), and a

heart that needs to be controlled by the Holy Spirit (Rom 12:6-21; Gal 5:19-26).

ADHD - Comorbidity

When clinicians diagnose a child to be ADHD, they typically also

diagnose a comorbid disorder.[119] All of the behaviors that are qualified as ADHD

criteria in the *DSM* are found in other disorders and diseases. This reality led Dr.

Richard Saul to conclude that ADHD does not exist. He believes, "Comorbid

conditions are in fact the only cause of distractibility and impulsivity

symptoms."[120] In contrast to Saul, other secularists see the associated behaviors

as indicating comorbidity with ADHD rather than explaining away the disorder.

The most frequent comorbid diagnosis of ADHD appearing in approximately

half all diagnoses is Oppositional-Defiant Disorder (ODD).[121] In fact, many

believe ADHD and ODD are inseparable diagnoses:

> Most hyperactive children manifest interpersonal behavior that has several distinct characteristics: (1) a considerable resistance to social demands, a resistance to "do's" and "don'ts," to "shoulds" and "shouldn'ts"; (2) increased independence; (3) domineering behavior with other children. *Probably the single most disturbing feature of ADHD children's behavior, and the one most frequently responsible for their referral for treatment is the difficulty many of these children have in complying with requests and prohibitions of parents and teachers.* [emphasis added] Some ADHD children may appear almost impossible to discipline. In some respects they seem to remain two years old.[122]

---

[119] Bruce Pennington, *Diagnosing Learning Disorders: A Neuropsychological Framework,* 2nd d. (New York: Guilford, 2009), 155.

[120] Richard Saul, *ADHD Does Not Exist: The Truth about Attention Deficit and Hyperactivity Disorder* (New York: HarperCollins, 2014), 14.

[121] *DSM,* 88.

[122] Wender, *ADHD,* 24-25.

Barkley informs parents to expect ODD behaviors with ADHD and describes to

parents what to watch for:

> often loses control of temper, often disputes or argues with adults, often actively rebels against or refuses adults' rules or requests, often deliberately does things that annoy other people, often blames others for own misdeeds, often easily irked or annoyed by others, often resentful and angry, and often spiteful or revengeful.[123]

Barkley's description of ODD and ADHD accurately depicts the biblical

understanding of the "ordinary fool"[124] and, in some cases, the scoffer depicted

in Proverbs. Though most children diagnosed with ADHD may not be ordinary

fools or scoffers, all children begin as simple fools in need of divine wisdom

(refer to appendix A). When left to their naturally foolish way of thinking apart

from the gospel, these children will become full-fledged fools.

No matter how secularists attempt to categorize and label children, God's

remedy for man's sinful nature is the same across all humanity. Though the

depraved hearts of children labeled with ADHD are not peculiar, these children

express their foolish hearts in more frequent and observable behaviors. Of

course, God is just as concerned about the quiet rebel whose foolishness is

hidden in the heart as he is about the child whose self-centeredness is more

external. Both types of children need to experience salvation and grow in

sanctification to produce a new heart that pleases God. The product of a heart

changed by divine wisdom will be prudent behavior that is beneficial to both the

child and his community.[125]

---

[123] *TCoA*, 169.

[124] Kidner, *Proverbs*, 39-41.

[125] Waltke, *1-15*, 177.

It is important to note that in spite of secularists' admission that the *DSM* criteria for ADHD are normal behaviors, they still insist that the distinction between normal and abnormal is the frequency and repetition of behavior.[126] Scripture, however, judges frequent and repetitive misbehavior to be expected from the foolish heart: "Like a dog that returns to his vomit is a fool who repeats his folly" (Prov 26:11).[127] The more foolish a child's heart becomes, the more frequent will be his foolish behavior even to the point that his life can eventually be dominated by his sin (Ps 119:133; Rom 6:11-14).[128] Secularists often refer to this reality as addiction. Jay Adams remarks on the direct application of Proverbs 26:11 for parents: "To rescue a fool out of the consequences of his sin is unproductive. It does him little good. Unless the underlying pattern of foolish behavior and thought is replaced by a biblical pattern, the fool will repeat his

---

[126] *TCoA*, 9.

[127] "In both the image and the topic, the body rejects the repulsive object (i.e., vomit and folly), but the debased spirit craves it!" (Waltke, *1-15*, 354). Kidner notes, "[Second] Peter 2:22 quotes this to show that by this action such a person gives himself away" (*Proverbs*, 163). Likewise, Longman writes, "One of the characteristics of fools is their unwillingness to listen to correction. They make mistakes, but since they will not listen to criticism, they are doomed to repeat those mistakes" (467). The repetition of foolishness reveals the foolish heart.

[128] Psychotherapists do not use the term *sin* but do recognize that pursuits and substances can dominate an individual's life and refer to those dominated by sin as *addicts*. All sin, not just addictive substances seeks to dominate and master mankind. Jay Adams writes concerning Romans 6:11-14 that "the desires of sin, habituated in the body by years of service to sin, will be to do unrighteousness. So sin must no longer be obeyed. Its desires (that over time have become habitual desires of the body) will tend in the wrong direction. Your body (which includes the brain, programmed by your sinful nature) will desire to do sinful things that you know you must not do" (*Christian Counselor's Commentary: Romans, Philippians, 1 and 2 Thessalonians* [Hackettstown, N.J.: Timeless Texts, 1995], 53). Psalm 119:133, however, offers the remedy to repetition of foolishness. Boice writes, "Though sin is a master and seeks to destroy, the word of God can "give direction for [one's] footsteps, victory over sin, and salvation from those who have been trying to destroy him (vv. 133-4)" (James Montgomery Boice, *Psalms 107-50*, vol. 3 of *Psalms*, Expositional Commentary [Grand Rapids: Baker, 1998], 1043).

folly."[129] Simply addressing behaviors, then, whether through behaviorism or medicine, will never remedy the child's core problem.

Biblically Discuss the Cause of Behavior

Unlike secular theories based on evolutionary thought, Scripture declares that man's heart controls his behaviors and is his greatest problem.[130] Solomon emphasized to his son the need to guard his heart since from the heart proceed the issues of life (4:23).[131] Solomon's deliberate choice of words depicts a city gate in Scripture which controls traffic and illustrates how the heart controls behavior (Prov 4:23-27).[132] The gate of the heart controls the mouth (24), the eyes (21, 25), the feet (26-27), and the ears (20) – the very things those with the ADHD label appear to be unable to control. Yet while the heart controls behavior, behaviors ultimately control the heart. In other words, the afore-mentioned behaviors

---

[129] Adams, *CCC Proverbs*, 199.

[130] Peter Steveson writes about guarding the heart (Prov 4:23) that "the concern for the keeping of one's own mind [heart] should transcend any other self-protecting act. This is so because the mind is the source of every thought, every word, and every action of man" (63).

[131] Longman sees the comparison between Proverbs 4:23 and 3:1. The child is to protect or guard his heart. This is not merely a defensive position against wrong doctrine, but a protection of the stored wisdom (to ponder). He states, "Protection means to observe the commands that are to be deeply embedded in the son." This also reveals that guarding or protecting the heart means to remember or keep in mind to the point of obedience (131). See also Adams, *CCC Proverbs*, 42.

[132] Waltke notes that cartographers used the word to describe "'exits' of a city" such as in Ezekiel 48:30, and he also notes other usages such as the psalmist's use in describing his escape in Psalm 68:20 which lead him to conclude: "The point here is that the heart is the source of the body's activities" (1-15, 298). Similarly, Whybray translates "from it flow the springs" as "literally, 'the outgoings' of life" (R.N. Whybray, *Proverbs*, New Century Bible Commentary [Grand Rapids: InterVarsity, 1996], 82). Kidner also notes that the issues of life are those things which both enter the man (20-22) and flow out of the man ("'the outgoings'; RSV: *the springs*") (*Proverbs*, 68).

(namely seeing and hearing), shape man's heart/character. Waltke recognizes

this paradox:

> Since the heart is the center of all the person's emotional-intellectual-religious-moral activity, it must be safe-guarded above all things (4:23). Paradoxically, the eye and ear are gates to the heart and shape it (see 2:2; 4:21-23;), but at the same time the heart decides what they will hear and see (4:25-26).[133]

The New Testament also recognizes the heart as responsible and the source of all its own behaviors: "what comes out of the mouth proceeds from the heart, and this defiles a person" (Matt 15:18). Ryle emphasizes, "With respect to the human heart our Lord declares in these verses that it is the true source of all sin and defilement."[134] Behavior is always sourced in man's heart, rather than in genetics or neurological defects, and thus each man is responsible for not only what he allows into his heart, but also how he behaves.

The Desires of Man's Heart Control His Behaviors

Since man's heart controls his behaviors, it follows that his desires both control his heart and reveal it. Matthew 6:19-23 illustrates this truth: "For where your treasure is, there your heart will be also. The eye is the lamp of the body. So, if your eye is healthy, your whole body will be full of light, but if your eye is bad, your whole body will be full of darkness. If then the light in you is darkness, how great is the darkness (21-23)." Hendriksen and Kistemaker explain these verses:

> Implication on the basis of verses 19–21: Just as a person has a natural eye (the *one* eye representing both eyes here) to illumine his physical existence and to bring him into contact with his earthly environment, so he has a spiritual eye, namely, the mind, to brighten his inner life, to guide him morally and spiritually, and to keep him in contact

---

[133] Waltke, *1-15*, 92.

[134] Ryle, 128.

with the heavenly Father. But if the "light" that is in him be darkened — for example, by means of his inordinate yearning for earthly treasure —, then how great must be that darkness, the very organ of light-reception having been obscured by sin. By missing what should have been his goal, namely, the promotion of God's glory, this person misses everything!

The impossibility of combining two opposite goals (glorifying God and satisfying the yearnings of the flesh) is stated very tersely and unambiguously in verse 24. **No one can serve two masters; for either he will hate the one and love the other, or he will be devoted to one and look down on the other. You cannot serve God and Mammon.** The man with the misplaced *heart* (verse 21) and misdirected *mind* (verses 22 and 23) also suffers from a misaligned *will,* a will not in line with God's will (verse 24). He i*mag*ines, perhaps, that he can give his full allegiance to the two goals of glorifying God and acquiring material possessions, but he errs. He will either hate the one and love the other, or vice versa.[135]

The desires of the heart reveal the individuals goals, determine his lifestyle, and ultimately determine his destination.

The true problem that children labelled as ADHD have is a value system that fails to consider God's glory and their own destiny. Even secularists recognize that the nature of every child is to "want what he wants when he wants it. He acts without reflection or consideration of the consequences."[136] The heart of a child diagnosed with ADHD, like those of all unregenerate children, rebels against right desires, right values, and right motives.

Man is Responsible for His Behaviors

Because man's heart controls his behavior, man is responsible for all that he does. Whereas clinicians' use of the ADHD label attempts to justify a child's natural idolatrous desires and pursuits, the biblical perspective of the same tendencies holds the child fully responsible for his actions and reveals the destructive error of his misplaced worship.

---

[135] William Hendriksen and Simon J. Kistemaker, *Exposition of the Gospel According to Matthew*, vol. 9 of New Testament Commentary (Grand Rapids: Baker, 2012), 347–48.

[136] Wender, *ADHD*, 15.

Moreover, the reality that God is man's authority and deserves man's attention and obedience requires man to give an account to God for all that he does, especially regarding his authority (Rom 13:1-5). God's authority is established in the humbling reality that he is man's creator (Rom 1:20-21) and the judge of man's actions and motives (Rom 2:1-8). Man must either choose to fear the Lord in humility or naturally embrace arrogant self-worship, yet both choices require that man give an account to God. Though man's deceptive heart excels at providing excuses for his sinful desires and behaviors, God's perfect judgment considers man's excuses invalid.

Every Heart Needs Christ's Redemption

The greatest gift to a child struggling with sinful behavior is God's grace that brings salvation and enables sanctification (Ti 2:11-15). The transforming power of grace changes both the inward man and the outward man even to the core issue of his desires. Though God created man in his own image, sin has marred this image and left man falling short of God's glory (Rom 3:10, 23). In the sense that every man falls short of God's glory, created image, and intended purpose, every natural man is abnormal and set against God. God's grace alone can supply the power to save and to sanctify the heart (Eph 1-3) and enable righteous relationships and God-pleasing behavior (Eph 4-6).[137]

---

[137] In the first three chapters of Ephesians, Paul establishes God's ability alone to save and sanctify sinners. In the last three chapters, Paul discusses how God's sanctification is practically lived out in relationships with God and man (Foulkes, 20).

Man's Heart Leads to Destructive Consequences

Apart from divine wisdom and left to follow its natural inclinations and desires, the heart of man will incur destructive consequences. Scripture reveals that these consequences are both temporal and eternal in nature and that they reemphasize man's need of Christ's redemption.

Emotional and Social Consequences

Without grace, many people live lives of unfulfilled desires and loneliness (Prov 14:14). Unlike the wise son who humbly fears the Lord and is given "riches, honor, and life" (Prov 22:4), the one who is foolish is unhappy (Prov 8:32, 34) and more likely to use substances[138] in adulthood in search of satisfaction (Prov 20:1). The foolish child also desires honor, yet his life is often characterized by social disgrace and shame (Prov 3:35; 13:18), and his foolish behavior incites conflicts[139] and brings his parents sorrow.[140]

The relational problems associated with the ADHD construct result in frustration and pain both for the child or adult given the ADHD label and for that individual's loved ones. Scripture indicates that fornication can be eventually characteristic of a foolish heart (Prov 5; 7:5-23). Secular studies reveal that adults diagnosed with ADHD have worse marriages and engage in higher

---

[138] *TCoA*, 80; Elissa P. Benedek, review of *ADHD in Adults: What the Science Says*, by Russell A. Barkley, Kevin Murphy, and Mariellen Fischer. *Bulletin of the Menninger Clinic* 73, no. 1 (Winter 2009): 69-74. See also Gabrielle Weiss and Lily Trokenberg Hechtman, *Hyperactive Children Grown Up: ADHD in Children, Adolescents, and Adults*, 2nd ed. (New York: Guilford, 1993), 133-35.

[139] Weiss and Hechtman, 25-26.

[140] Prov 10:1; 17:25; 23:15; 24-25.

rates of promiscuity than those considered normal in society.[141] In addition, the foolish child also affects the relationships of those around him. Barkley notes, "Parents of children with ADHD also report . . . more marital or couple problems than other parents."[142]

Shorter Life and Antisocial Behavior

Scripture also addresses the temporal life of those who continue to pursue their own way and reject wisdom. Fools live a shorter life than God desires for them (Prov 3:2-3)[143] as their heart's "craving for attention, impulsivity, and tendency to not 'plan ahead'"[144] invite harmful consequences and dangerous situations. The fool takes risks as his lustful and proud heart makes him feel invincible and incites conflicts that may even lead to bloodshed (Prov 13:2-3; Jas 4:1-3). Secular studies verify that antisocial and criminal behaviors (such as conflicts with police, fighting, stealing, and destructiveness) are higher in children labelled as having ADHD.[145] Though God does not promise that the righteous man will live longer than the fool, he does issue the sober warning that foolish and disobedient behavior leads to physical and spiritual death. Clearly, research reaffirms the validity of Scripture and the need for man to accept God's remedy.

---

[141] Barkley, Russell A., Kevin R. Murphy, and Mariellen Fischer, *ADHD in Adults: What the Science Says* (New York: Guilford, 2008), 500.

[142] Ibid. This statistic could also indicate that the parents' poor relationship is influencing the child rather than the child's behavior influencing his parents' marriage.

[143] See also Ephesians 6:1-3, Waltke, *1-15*, 240-41, and Steveson, 37-38.

[144] Wender, *ADHD*, 27.

[145] Weiss and Hechtman, 85.

Spiritual Death

Although the temporal consequences of foolish behavior are sobering, the eternal consequences are far greater. This fact should compel counselors, teachers, and parents to teach children that apart from grace, the human heart seeks its own destructive way (Rom 2:1-11; 6:20-23), and this pursuit brings condemnation (Prov 12:2). Since the heart is naturally set against God, the destiny of every foolish man is eternal death and separation from God (Prov 8:35-36; Rom 6:23). It is only through God's grace, displayed in Christ's atoning work on the cross, that foolish men can know and submit to God's way and that the Holy Spirit can accomplish the work of salvation through faith in Christ alone (Eph 2:1-10). Though foolishness is entwined into the nature of every child, Scripture provides the solution of hope and deliverance which can drive foolishness far from the child's heart (Prov 22:15)[146] and enable right living through God's wisdom (Prov 1:2-5).

Conclusion

Though the behaviors associated with ADHD are not the primary focus in parenting or discipleship, behavior must be addressed since according to Scripture, it has moral value (pleasing or displeasing to God) and it is each child's responsibility. Furthermore, behavior exposes every person's greatest problem: a depraved heart needing Christ's redemption. By scripturally and lovingly addressing these behaviors, parents, teachers, and counselors confront the child with the sufficiency of God's Word, which exposes the true nature of human depravity but also reveals the good and loving nature of God. The child's

---

[146] William McKane, *Proverbs: A New Approach* (Philadelphia: Westminster, 1970), 564-65.

exposure to Scripture provides him with the choice either to continue foolishly trusting in his own self-destructive wisdom or to humbly place his faith in the transforming wisdom of God that brings hope and deliverance. Though parents should desire their child's behavior to positively change, they must remain focused on the child's greatest needs and trust the work of God in their child's heart to accomplish this need. [147]

---

[147] Tedd Tripp, *Shepherding a Child's Heart* (Wapwallopen, Pa.: Shepherd Press, 1995), 4-6.

CHAPTER 3 – MEETING THE CHILD'S GREATEST NEEDS

Although the child's circumstances and physical maladies do undoubtedly influence his decisions and behavior,[1] everyone has underlying spiritual needs that only Scripture can address. In fact, every child needs either to be saved or to progress further in personal sanctification. This reality is the child's greatest need and requires that parents accurately discern the child's relationship with God and biblically deal with his or her spiritual needs.

The Need to Trust in God's Wisdom

Reaching the heart is a delicate business that will demand both a rejection of human understanding (including secular theories) and a deep commitment to God's wisdom. In fact, Proverbs 28:26 declares that anyone who trusts in his own heart is a fool, but the one who walks wisely will be delivered. Deliverance, then, only comes through God's wisdom. Secular wisdom contends that ADHD is a child's "inability to self-regulate,"[2] but it rejects the idea that a child's own depravity and the absence of God's wisdom are causes of the lack of restraint.

---

[1] Garrett Higbee, "'Tony' and Bipolar Disorder," in *Counseling the Hard Cases: True Stories Illustrating the Sufficiency of God's Resources in Scripture,* ed. Stuart Scott and Heath Lambert (Nashville: B&H Publishing Group, 2012), 174.

[2] Russell A. Barkley, *ADHD and the Nature of Self-Control* (New York: Guilford, 2005), 47-64. Hereafter referred to as *NoSC.*

Scripture, however, teaches that as people pursue selfish ambitions which are in opposition to God's purposes, they will experience undesirable consequences: "Where jealousy and selfish ambition exist, there will be disorder and every vile practice" (Jas 3:16). Proverbs 29:18 states that "where there is no prophetic vision the people cast off restraint, but blessed is he who keeps the law." This proverb speaks directly to child rearing, and when understood properly this verse explains many of the unrestrained behaviors in society.[3] Waltke argues that without acquiring the guiding power of divine wisdom, society[4] will "fall into anarchy."

These passages clearly indicate that when Scripture is absent from a child's moral education, the disorder and lack of self-control bound in every child's heart will emerge and even affect society.[5] Without the restraint of God's grace and wisdom,[6] a child's life will be marked by relational hardships and self-

---

[3] Waltke states that Proverbs 29:18 is "another rearing proverb, [which] turns for a moment from the family and the son to the community's need of wisdom" (Bruce K. Waltke, *The Book of Proverbs: Chapters 15-30*, New International Commentary on the Old Testament, ed. R. K. Harrison and Robert L. Hubbard Jr. [Grand Rapids: Eerdmans, 2005], 445).

[4] Waltke's connection of child-rearing and the community's need of wisdom is both because of the context as well as the reality that children are the next society (ibid., 445-46).

[5] Though secularists do not blame a child's lack of self-control on his depraved heart, they do identify children diagnosed with ADHD to lack self-control (Paul Wender, *ADHD: Attention-Deficit Hyperactivity Disorder in Children, Adolescents, and Adults* [New York: Oxford University Press, 2000], 27).

[6] Erickson defines God's wisdom as "acting in the light of all of the facts and of correct values." Those who receive God's wisdom act in truth and view life as God does (Millard J. Erickson, *Christian Theology*, 2nd ed. [Grand Rapids: Baker, 1999], 301). Kidner sees divine wisdom in Proverbs consisting of five parts: (1) instruction or training (2) understanding or insight (3) good sense or practical wisdom (4) shrewdness or discretion (5) knowledge and learning, which is to know God (*Proverbs*, 36-37).

destructive behaviors (whether observable or not). Therefore, all discipline must stem from God's wisdom to effectively address a child's heart (Prov 1:8).

The Sufficiency of God's Word

In contrast to secular proposals which fail to offer permanent solutions for a child's behavioral problems, the timeless truth of Scripture offers hope. This wonderful news is possible because Scripture is uniquely designed by God to reveal himself and to address man's behavioral, spiritual/mental, and relational problems. In other words, Christ came to restore man to his intended state of holiness through the true knowledge of Himself and the regeneration by the Holy Spirit. It is not surprising then, that God's revelation is perfect, sure, right, clear, pure, true, all-together righteous, and everlasting; it enables the restoration of man's soul, makes man wise, causes a glad heart, and provides enlightenment in all issues of life (Ps 19:7-9). Second Peter 1:3 crystallizes the biblical claim that the true knowledge of God is sufficient to address all of life's issues, including the patterns of behaviors that secularists label as ADHD. Ed Welch writes,

> Given the degree to which God has revealed himself and ourselves, we can assume that the Bible's counsel speaks with great breadth, addressing the gamut of problems in living. It is certainly able to speak to the common problems we all encounter, such as relationship conflicts, financial pressures, our responses to physical health or illness, parenting questions, and loneliness. But it also speaks to distinctly modern problems such as depression, anxiety, mania, schizophrenia and attention deficit disorder, just to name a few. Of course, the Bible doesn't speak to each of these problems as would an encyclopedia. It doesn't offer techniques for change that look like they came out of a cookbook. But through prayerful meditation on Scripture and a willingness to receive theological guidance from each other, we find that the biblical teaching on creation, the fall, and redemption provide specific, useful insight into all the issues of life.[7]

---

[7] Ed Welch, "What Is Biblical Counseling, Anyway," *Journal of Biblical Counseling* 16, no. 1 (1997): 3.

In spite of the Bible's claim to be sufficient to meet man's spiritual needs, many believers view issues that secularists label mental disorders as falling outside of the sufficiency of Scripture. Here again lies the choice between faith in man and faith in God: embracing the conclusion that mental disorders demand modern secular treatments alone requires faith as does a commitment to the sufficiency of the Scriptures to diagnose and remedy these heart issues.

The Reliability of God's Word

Not only is the Word of God sufficient to meet the relational needs in each family, it is also reliable. In contrast to ever-changing secular views on ADHD, secular labels, and diagnostic criteria, God's declarations are immutable (Heb 6:17-18) and everlasting (Ps 119:89), with their vantage point being his perfect knowledge (Prov 2:6). God's Word is the essential source of immutable truth that objectively provides reliable answers and is able to deliver us from our depraved heart and sinful behaviors. Furthermore, Scripture consistently discerns and addresses man's behavior, his morality, and his motives (Heb 4:12-13). Guthrie writes, "Nothing, not even our innermost thoughts, is shielded from the discernment of the message of God. It affects in a most comprehensive manner the whole man."[8] In light of the Scripture's sufficiency to answer and reliability to remedy, the wise counselor or parent will trust its explanation and solution for each child's heart and behavioral issues.

---

[8] Guthrie, *Hebrews*, 122-23.

The Need to Hope in Christ

Unlike secular theories of behavior, Scripture offers genuine hope of lasting change for each family. The apostle Paul writes, "For whatever was written in former days was written for our instruction, that through endurance and the encouragement of the Scriptures we might have hope" (Rom 15:4). Paul points out in this passage that Scripture is both the revelation of God's instruction to believers as well as the source of genuine hope. In light of this truth, Jay Adams stresses that it is the work of the Holy Spirit (Rom 5:13b) through the Word of God that offers hope to mankind.[9]

One example of such biblical change is found in Titus 3:1-8, where Paul gives testimony of the power of God's goodness to save men from both eternal condemnation and sinful behaviors. Although Paul does not list specific ADHD behaviors in his letter, he does judge the church members' behaviors prior to conversion to be foolish, disobedient, deceived, lustful, and self-indulgent (Ti 3:3). Bruce emphasizes that Paul's use of the words *malice* and *envy* indicated the "anti-social nature" of the behaviors of their past lives prior to conversion.[10] Proverbs records similar wording in describing many of the same behaviors that secularists now label as criteria of ADHD. Paul's remedy for these heart conditions and outworking behaviors was not man's abilities, efforts, sciences, or medications but rather the completed work of Christ on the cross (5-7). The believers' hearts on Crete changed according to their faith and produced behaviors that were not carnal or anti-social but rather "good works" that were

---

[9] "Spiritual Counseling Is Spiritual," *Bibliotheca Sacra* 131 (Oct 74): 292-94.

[10] Bruce, 254.

"good and profitable unto men" (8). Scriptural examples such as this provide us with hope in the power of the Holy Spirit, the completed work of Christ on the cross, and the immutable Word of God to produce similar changes in all of us.

The Need to Depend upon the Holy Spirit's Work of Change

Biblical change occurs through the vital work of the Holy Spirit through the Scriptures.[11] It is the Spirit's ministry, using the believer's faithfulness, which can bring about regeneration, righteous heart changes, and corresponding wise behavior.[12] Specifically, the Holy Spirit enables a child to understand God's wisdom (1 Cor 2:1-16), and He empowers the believer to make right changes (Rom 8:13; Eph 3:14-17). Furthermore, he intercedes on our behalf (Rom 8:26-27), and he actively sanctifies those who place their faith in him.

The Need to be a Disciple of Christ

Although the Holy Spirit produces salvation and sanctification, all believing parents have the God-given responsibility to actively participate in guiding their children toward becoming disciples of Christ.[13] Scripture presents three basic elements of discipline or discipleship: exemplifying, illustrating, and teaching/correcting. First, Scripture consistently features godly parents or authorities who exemplify the godly character that they desire their children to possess. Additionally, Scripture teaches that parents must provide verbal and

---

[11] *Competent to Counsel: Introduction to Nouthetic Counseling* (Grand Rapids: Zondervan, 1970), 20.

[12] Charles H. Spurgeon, *An All-Round Ministry* (London: Banner of Truth, 1960), 8-9.

[13] "Parenting children with ADD symptoms is ultimately like parenting any child: you tailor your biblical instruction to the child's abilities" (Edward T. Welch, *A.D.D. Wandering Minds and Wired Bodies* [Phillipsburg, N.J.: P&R, 1999], 17).

physical illustrations that reinforce practical theology and address the child's naturally sinful nature. Finally, Scripture presents the teaching of biblical and practical theology (grace) as essential to discipleship. These applications of biblical discipline will encourage right changes in the heart of both parent and child, and these changes will in turn produce obedient behavior and a fulfilled life.

It is worth noting again the process by which a child is disciplined or educated as recorded in Proverbs 4:20-27. The three elements of biblical parental discipline (exemplifying, illustrating, and instructing/correcting) correspond with this understanding of how the heart is educated and how it produces the issues of life. Hubbard views Proverbs 4:20-27 as emphasizing what he calls the "anatomy of discipleship."[14] The author of Proverbs shifts directions from explaining the two ways in which a child can choose to live (wisely or foolishly) to discussing how the child is educated.[15] Kidner notes that this is much like a medical inspection "in which one's state of readiness in the various realms symbolized by heart, mouth, eyes, [ears], and feet, comes under review."[16] The elements of parental discipline that will be presented, then, must speak directly to or influence these receptive parts of the child. Whether it is through seeing their parent's lifestyle (the child's eyes engaged and the parent's feet in practice), or hearing their parents instructions (the child's ears engaged and the parent's mouth in action), God designed the human body to receive information to

---

[14] D. A. Hubbard, *Proverbs* (Dallas: Word, 1989), 87.

[15] Waltke, *1-15*, 294.

[16] Kidner, *Proverbs*, 68.

educate the heart. It is imperative, then, for individuals to guard their hearts and children learn to do so by observing at close range their authorities guarding their hearts.

Although numerous Scripture references give parental wisdom which is applicable to the ADHD label, Proverbs 3 is one passage that provides both a framework of biblical parental discipline/discipleship and practical theology within the parent/child relationship.[17] In fact, Kidner calls chapter 3 "the whole-hearted disciple,"[18] and in chapter 4, Solomon calls this wisdom from the previous chapter and the entire book "good teaching" that should be passed down through generations (Prov 4:2-4). The first part of chapter 3 (1-12) reads like a covenant between God and man. Waltke emphasizes that the odd verses list the obligations of the son or disciple (the human participant), and the even verses reveal God's detailed commitment to the covenant.[19] The father's giving this wisdom, which he calls his own, indicates his desire to see his son enter into a covenant relationship with God and thus become a disciple of God.

Proverbs offers not only practical truths for the home but also desirable outcomes and hope to children who receive, retain, and live out God's wisdom. Children who embrace wise teaching can find hope in the promise of a good, long, and peaceable life (3:2) as well as in the prospect of finding favor with

---

[17] One of the key counseling points that Ed Welch offers to parents with a child labelled as having ADHD is to "become an expert in the book of Proverbs" (Welch, A.D.D., 13).

[18] Kidner, Proverbs, 63.

[19] Bruce Waltke, "Does Proverbs Promise Too Much?" Andrews University Seminary Studies 34 (1996): 319-36.

others (3:4).[20] However, the primary motive that must drive parents or children to pursue and keep God's wisdom is the desire for an intimate covenant relationship with God. Solomon expresses this underlying motive as the desire "to find favor and good success in the sight of God" (3:4).[21] Like Christ (Lk 2:40, 52), the child who pursues wisdom will be growing in grace and be pleasing to God and those around him.[22]

Right Patterning – Proverbs 3:1b-2

Throughout Scripture, the central component of godly discipline is the learner's observation of his teacher's genuine relationship with God. Though having godly models does not guarantee that a child will follow his parents' teaching, the parents' own lives are key aspects of biblical authoritative discipline. The father in Proverbs is one example of a parent who exhorts his son both to accept his spiritual teaching as well as to observe his ways (Prov 23:26). McKane writes, "'Let your eyes observe my ways' means simply, 'Take my life as a paradigm.'"[23] Proverbs 24:32 states the same idea but from the child's perspective: "Then I saw and considered it; I looked and received instruction." McKane comments on this verse, "Here is a new way of accepting *musar* [discipline]—not by paying attention to the authoritative [verbal] instruction of a

---

[20] Waltke sees Proverbs 3:1-12 revealing three key conditional blessings of receiving divine wisdom: (1) *social favor* (3:4), (2) *straight paths* (3:6b), and (3) *health* (3:8) (*1-15*, 238).

[21] Favor should be understood as the common word for "grace" (ibid., 242). See also Kidner, *Proverbs*, 63 and Longman, 132-33.

[22] Longman writes, "The reward, therefore, of obedience is that God and fellow human beings will respect such a person for having grace and good favor. They will be honored and sought after for their wisdom" (133).

[23] William McKane, *Proverbs: A New Approach* (Philadelphia: Westminster, 1970), 389-90.

teacher and acting on his advice, but by direct observation, followed by reflection, then conviction."[24] The New Testament reiterates the same principle of modelling: "A disciple is not above his teacher, but everyone when he is *fully trained*[25] will be like his teacher" (Lk 6:40).[26] Similarly, *Baker Encyclopedia of the Bible* defines a disciple as "someone who follows another person or another way of life and who submits himself to the discipline (teaching) of that leader or way."[27] Discipline, then, begins with modeling. Even secular advocates of the ADHD theory acknowledge that a parent's mindset and lifestyle are powerful influences in teaching children:

> Important to note but often unspecified in modern neuropsychological conceptualizations of working memory is that this ability [imitation] underlies the imitation of complex sequences of behavior by individuals. Imitation is a powerful tool by which humans learn new behaviors. The power to imitate another person's behavior requires the capacity to retain a mental representation of the behavior to be imitated. In many cases, that representation will be made through visual imagery or covert audition.[28]

---

[24] Ibid., 572; Waltke agrees: "The father probably emphasizes that 'I' did this to serve as a model to his son whom he instructed in his prologue to do the same (see 1:2-3; 22:17)" (*15-31*, 299-300).

[25] *Fully trained* (καταρτίζω) means to restore, to render fit, complete, or recreate (Leon Morris, *Luke: An Introduction and Commentary*, vol. 3, Tyndale New Testament Commentaries Downers Grove: InterVarsity, 1988], 153). When godly discipleship is complete, it brings about restoration or re-creation into the teacher's image. Therefore the believing parent should increasingly resemble his Creator as the parent progresses in sanctification.

[26] "Tenderly and lovingly the Master now assures them that although they will never be able to outrank or surpass him, yet thorough training under his direction will, if they accept it, cause them to become like their Teacher; that is, like him not in degree of knowledge or wisdom but in truly reflecting his image to the world, so that people instructed by them will begin to say, 'We can notice that these men have been with Jesus' (see Acts 4:13b)" (William Hendriksen and Simon J. Kistemaker, *Exposition of the Gospel According to Luke*, vol. 11 of New Testament Commentary [Grand Rapids: Baker, 2012], 361).

[27] Walter A. Elwell, ed., *Baker Encyclopedia of the Bible* (Grand Rapids: Baker, 1997), 630-31.

[28] *NoSC*, 164.

Godly parents, however, are not to provide their children with merely good teaching or an outward display of right behavior, but are to manifest godly behavior from a heart that loves God (Deut 6:1-7). Thompson comments on Deuteronomy 6: "*You shall love Yahweh your God. Israel's obedience was not to spring from a barren legalism based on necessity and duty. It was to arise from a relationship based on love.*"[29] In truth, becoming a good parent means growing more in love with God and knowing him more intimately. Because of the dramatic effect that a parent's lifestyle has on a child, parents must carefully consider their own attitudes, behaviors and pursuits. Such examination may reveal that the child with the ADHD label is only imitating the attitudes and lifestyle displayed at home.

Wise Discipline

So what does wise discipline look like? In Proverbs 3:1, Solomon warns his son, "Forget not my teaching, but let your heart keep my commandments." Though Solomon was exhorting his son to receive God's wisdom, he identified this teaching as his own.[30] It is important to reiterate that the Word of God must be central both to life and to the biblical discipline in the home. Proverbs 1:8

---

[29] J. A. Thompson, *Deuteronomy: An Introduction and Commentary*, vol. 5 of Tyndale Old Testament Commentaries, ed. Donald J. Wiseman (Downers Grove: InterVarsity, 1974), 138.

[30] Longman, 131. Of the same wording elsewhere in Proverbs, Longman states, "The specific teacher appropriates the accumulated wisdom of the tradition as his own in order to pass it on to his disciple" (415). Kidner views the personal pronoun *my* as signifying that these teachings were divine maxims taught in the home. Divine truth was an integral part of who the family was (*Proverbs*, 63). Though the instructions were divine, the father was the mouthpiece (Waltke, *1-15*, 240). Waltke says of Proverbs 2:1, a similar grammatical construction, that the idea is "an anthropomorphism that suggest that the father's mouth is a surrogate of God's mouth" (Ibid., 224). Since the heart speaks through the mouth, what the father spoke revealed his heart for God.

connects both the unity of the father and mother and the unity of their discipline (*musar*) with the revelation of God (*Torah*). Most commentators note that the father and mother act as one flesh and the parents discipline and the revelation of God collaborate to produce a wise child.[31] In fact, in commenting on Proverbs 13:1, Smith notes this truth: "'A wise son [is] discipline of a father.' To make sense of this clause, NIV supplies the verb 'heeds,' NASB 'accepts.' The meaning is that on account of a father's discipline the son is wise."[32] This should be understood as the way to achieve the goal of a wise son is to discipline him. Likewise, the Jewish commentator, Cohen notes,

> The Hebrew is literally "a wise son discipline of a father." A.AV. "a wise son heareth his father's instructions" supplies the verb from the second clause. Rashi offers two explanations: verbs like 'ask and loves' have to be understood; or, the meaning is that on account of the father's discipline the son is wise. The latter agrees better with the text: "a son is wise (as the effect of) a father's discipline."[33]

Right patterning must begin with a progressing relationship with God (Jn 15:1-17)[34] that then produces godly thinking and spiritual fruits (Gal 5:22-26). These right perspectives and behaviors are antithetical to the heart and behaviors of the unsaved, including those behaviors that characterize the ADHD construct.

> But I say, walk by the Spirit, and you will not gratify the desires of the flesh. For the desires of the flesh are against the Spirit, and the desires of the Spirit are against the flesh, for these are opposed to each other, to keep you from doing the things you want to do (Gal 5:16-17).

---

[31] Robert Harris, Gleason Archer Jr., and Bruce Waltke. Theological Wordbook of the Old Testament (Chicago: Moody Press, 2003), 387.

[32] James E. Smith, *The Wisdom Literature and Psalms*, Old Testament Survey Series (Joplin, MO: College Press Pub. Co., 1996), Prov 13:1.

[33] Abraham Cohen, *Proverbs* (London: Soncino Press, 1973), 80.

[34] Murdoch writes, "Change of being, *metanoia*, is not brought about by straining and 'will-power,' but a long deep process of unselfing" (Iris Murdoch, *Metaphysics as a Guide to Morals* [New York: Penguin, 1993], 52-54); f. Waltke, *1-15*, 221.

Only those walking in fellowship with God and under the Holy Spirit's control are able to demonstrate love, joy, peace, patience, kindness, goodness, faithfulness, gentleness, or self-control in a way that pleases God (22-23). These qualities sharply contrast with the impulsive, selfish, rude, disobedient, and uncontrolled behaviors that characterize the naturally depraved heart seeking to please itself. It is no wonder, then, that Scripture presents parental discipline as involving every aspect of a covenant relationship with God.[35] Biblical parental discipline that is patterned after right theology (Deuteronomy 8, Proverbs, and Hebrews 12) will offer the child insight/understanding, counsel, knowledge, correction, instruction in righteousness, so that the child can enter into the fear of the Lord and become wise/holy through the work of the Holy Spirit.

Foolish Instruction

One way to better understand wise discipline is to examine and address foolish parenting. Biblical discipline is more than verbal instruction; it is also a lifestyle. Proverbs 16:22 states, "Good sense is a fountain of life to him who has it, but the instruction [discipline] of fools [produces] folly." Clearly parents will either be a constant source of refreshing life for their children or lead them toward further foolishness;[36] no neutral ground exists.

---

[35] Kidner, *Proverbs*, 36-38.

[36] Breggin writes, "A growing body of psychological research confirms the obvious — that troubled families raise a high percentage of troubled children, who go on to become troubled adults" (Peter R. Breggin, *Toxic Psychiatry* [New York: St. Martin's Press, 1991], 273).

Destructive Behavior

The imitative nature of children almost guarantees that they will pursue and value the things their parents pursue and value. In contrast to God-fearing parents who desire above all to please the Lord, foolish parents seek their own pleasure and unwittingly point their children toward the same destructive mindsets and behaviors. In Ephesians 5:15, Paul reminds believers to "look carefully then how you walk, not as unwise but as wise." The documented existence of fighting, anger, and conflicts in families with children diagnosed with ADHD is one specific example of destructive modeling.[37] Secularists Hallowell and Ratey note, "ADD can drain a family. ADD can turn a family upside down and make everybody angry at everybody else."[38] Though secularists claim that alleged ADHD is to blame for a family's anger problems, Scripture explains that fighting, fits of anger, and familial conflicts are always caused by hearts that pursue their own pleasures and want their own ways (Jas 4:1-10). Ecclesiastes 7:9 admonishes the reader not to be "quick in your spirit to become angry, for anger lodges in the heart of fools." It is the self-centered nature of the heart and its propensity to hold on to anger permanently rather than genetics that are to blame for uncontrolled anger. In fact, parents should ask themselves specific questions about how they handle their own anger:

- How do you respond when life does not go your way?
- How do you respond when your family members irritate you?

---

[37] Edward M. Hallowell and John J. Ratey, *Delivered from Distraction: Getting the Most out of Life with Attention Deficit Disorder* (New York: Ballantine Books, 2005), 126-50.

[38] Ibid., 146.

- How do you respond when your children fail to meet your expectations?

Although parents may believe that their anger is justified, God's Word declares that "the anger of man does not produce the righteousness of God" (Jas 1:20). Not only do parental expressions of anger displease God, but parents' actions can also provoke a child's naturally selfish heart to be likewise wrathful (Eph 6:4a). Hodge writes:

> **Fathers, do not exasperate your children.** This is what they are not to do. They are not to excite the bad passions of their children by severity, injustice, partiality, or unreasonable exercise of authority. A parent would do better to sow weeds in a field from which he expects to derive food for himself and his family than by his own bad behavior to nurture evil in the heart of his child.[39]

Angry parents will most likely produce children who are also angry.[40] It is wrath that "stirs up strife" and anger that "causes much transgression" (Prov 29:22). Even secularists acknowledge that "immature, inexperienced, impulsive, inattentive, depressed, hostile, rejecting, or otherwise negatively temperamental parents are more likely to have defiant and aggressive children."[41]

In some homes, parents may have little conflict with their children, yet they fight openly and regularly with each other and expose their selfish hearts to their children. They slander their pastor, their child's teachers, and politicians in the privacy of their home. Other parents are self-deceived, believing that they are biblically disciplining their children, when in fact, they are provoking their

---

[39] Charles Hodge, *Ephesians*, vol. 7 of Crossway Classic Commentaries, ed. Alister McGrath and J. I. Packer (Wheaton: Crossway, 1994), 203.

[40] Peter R. Breggin, *Toxic Psychiatry* (New York: St. Martin's Press, 1991), 93.

[41] Russell A. Barkley, *Defiant Children: A Clinician's Manual for Assessment and Parent Training*, 2nd ed. (New York: Guilford, 1997), 40.

children to wrath with foolish reactions. These foolish choices undermine God's authority in the child's life and reveal a heart that will most likely motivate children to reject authority.

Destructive Influences

Of course parents and teachers are not the only influences children have; children must also deal with destructive influences outside the home. Though parents typically have the most influence in directing children's lives, Scripture also warns of godless people outside the home who set foolish examples and seek to lead the simple "in the way that is not good" (Prov 16:29). Proverbs 16:27-30 reveals the way in which a trouble-maker leads others astray with his mouth (whether intentionally or not): he insults (27), he gossips (28), he is aggressive (violent; 29), and he schemes (30).[42] Proverbs 11:9a provides a clear warning that "with his mouth the godless man would destroy his neighbor." These types of negative influences are prevalent in society, yet they have also infiltrated God-fearing homes by means of television, video games, music, movies, Internet, and other sources. Although the child is responsible for his own heart and behaviors, these influences can indoctrinate a child's thinking and promote foolishness.[43]

Parents must diligently protect their children from evil influences by overseeing all entertainment, friendships, and activities. Children should not have easy, unsupervised access to the Internet, television, and radio. Additionally, parents must actively monitor each child's friendships. If the child

---

[42] Kidner, *Proverbs*, 121.

[43] E.g., L. R. Huesmann, J. Moise-Titus, C. Podolski, and L. D. Eron, "Early Exposure to TV Violence Predicts Aggression in Adulthood"; available from http://www.apa.org/pi/prevent-violence/resources/tv-violence.aspx; Internet; accessed 15 August 2012.

is allowed to visit a friend's house, parents should be confident that they and the friend's family are like-minded and that the parents will be supervising all activities. Parental supervision may be hard and at times uncomfortable, but with the abundance of negative influences,[44] children need supervision more than ever.

Another prominent means by which Satan influences children is through the power of music.[45] Scripture reveals that music originates in a person's heart and thus it reveals the heart (Col 3:16). Not only can music reveal the heart, it can also move the heart farther away from God. God designed music as a unique means to communicate his wisdom to man and for man to communicate his worship to God,[46] but Satan desires to lead people away from God's wisdom, and music is one of his special tools.[47] Satan often influences children through the writers of godless music, yet unfortunately, many parents are unaware of or

---

[44] Chelsea Clinton and James P. Steyer, "Is the Internet Hurting Children?"; available from http://edition.cnn.com/2012/05/21/opinion/clinton-steyer-internet-kids/; Internet; accessed 2 January 2014. This article also points out the results of recent studies showing increased hyperactivity, difficulty focusing, and problems with comprehension in children who engage in too much multimedia content and hypertext.

[45] Through technological advances such as MP3 players, smart phones, and computers, music is more accessible and more influential than ever before.

[46] Garth Bolinder, Tom McKee, and John Cionca, *What Every Counselor Needs to Know about Music, Youth, and Education* (Waco, Tex.: CTI Word Books, 1986), 60-61. In contrast to worldly music that reflects the natural heart (Col 3:5-10), biblically centered music helps restore man's heart to the image of his Creator and promotes Christ as the object of man's highest value (Col 3:11-16). Music provides believers with a means of communicating their love, thankfulness, and honor to God. It can also indoctrinate believers with the mind of Christ and warn them against going their own way (Col 3:1-16).

[47] God created Lucifer to worship God with his musical ability, yet Satan's arrogant heart perverted the right worship of God by directing it toward himself. Because of Lucifer's arrogance, along with his self-worship, God expelled him from heaven while allowing him to retain his musical ability (Isa 14:11-12; Ez 28:11).

choose to ignore that "music reaches the depths of human personality in ways mere words never can."[48] Even some therapists who deal with ADHD understand the power of music to influence a child's mind, emotions, and behaviors,[49] and numerous secular musicians admit that their music is intended to influence the heart of the listener. For example, in her song *Music*, the singer Madonna repeats as her chorus, "Music makes the people come together; yeah, music makes the bourgeoisie and the rebels."[50] According to her words, music is powerful enough to influence those who listen to it to live a specific lifestyle. It also impacts the moral character: "Music can therefore ennoble or degrade character, make men better or worse than they are."[51] The power of music to influence the heart is evident,[52] yet many parents still permit foolish teachers to use their music to instruct their children toward the way that leads to death.[53]

---

[48] Bolinder, McKee, and Cionca, 60.

[49] Sandra F. Rief, *How to Reach and Teach ADD/ADHD Children: Practical Techniques, Strategies, and Interventions for Helping Children with Attention Problems and Hyperactivity* (West Nyack, N.Y.: Center for Applied Research in Education, 1993), 132-37.

[50] Madonna, "*Music*"; available from http://www.metrolyrics.com/music-lyrics-madonna.html; Internet.

[51] Julius Portnoy, *Music in the Life of Man* (New York: Holt, Rinehart and Winston, 1963), 6.

[52] In addition to mental responses, numerous studies reveal that various aspects of the body also respond to hearing music — dance is one example. For further examples, see Robert Lundin, *An Objective Psychology of Music* (New York: Ronald Press Co, 1953), 110. See also McDonald Critchey and R. A. Henson eds., *Music and the Brain: Studies in the Neurology of Music* (London: Heinemann Educational Books, 1977), 217-30.

[53] Though music can be a bad influence, it can also positively indoctrinate. Music can be useful tool for children who are struggling to remember things, and godly music can calm the child's spirit, develop his mind, and teach him biblical truth. For further study on how music can influence moods and mindsets and can even be used in counseling children, see chapter 8 of

In addition to monitoring their children's music choices, parents should prohibit their children's unsupervised use of electronic devices, especially those devices that could encourage aggression and violence.[54] Parents and teachers commonly observe verbal outbursts when others stand in way of the child diagnosed with ADHD.[55] Physical displays of violence and aggression also regularly occur,[56] but they must not be encouraged. In the same way that music can influence a child's heart, violent messages from video games, media, movies, Internet, and friends can also lead a child into further foolishness. These influences are pervasive in modern culture, and though they are not to blame for one's violence or bad behaviors, they can reinforce the natural bent of man's violent heart.[57] Therefore, parents must not allow violent influences to remain in their home. Instead they should carefully evaluate and supervise their children's lifestyles and forms of entertainment and eliminate those influences that are destructive and promote unacceptable behavior.

Carrie Anne Boyd, "The Role of Music in Counseling and Discipleship" (master's thesis, Master's College, 2002).

[54] It is worth noting that Scripture views violence not only as physical aggression against God and others (Ps 58:2), but as evidence of a destructive heart that is fixed on selfish pursuits (Jas 4:1-3).

[55] Wender, *ADHD*, 167.

[56] Ibid., 168.

[57] S. A. Ohene, M. Ireland, C. McNeely, and I.W. Borowsky, "Parental Expectations, Physical Punishment, and Violence among Adolescents Who Score Positive on a Psychosocial Screening Test in Primary Care," *Pediatrics* 117, no.6 (2006): 441-47.

Understandable Illustrations – Proverbs 3:3

In addition to providing children with patterns of godly behavior, parents must teach with thought-provoking illustrations. Fremont writes, "A superior teacher knows how to illustrate and simplify each truth he presents. The purpose of the illustration is to capture the attention of the listener and to motivate him to accept the idea presented."[58] God has designed all of creation to reveal his character and wisdom (Ps 19:1-6); therefore, counselors and parents are wise to use both verbal and physical illustrations to encourage the acceptance of vital truth. John Calvin says of Psalm 19:1-6:

> God is in himself invisible; but as his majesty shines forth in his works and in his creatures everywhere, men ought in these to acknowledge him, for they clearly set forth their Maker: and for this reason the Apostle in his Epistle to the Hebrews says, that this world is a mirror, or the representation of invisible things.[59]

The book of Proverbs, for example, teaches God's wisdom through imagery. Throughout the book Solomon uses illustrations, metaphors, and comparisons to teach his son the importance of fearing God and receiving his wisdom. "Proverbs . . . introduce[s] the reader to a style of teaching that provokes his thought, getting under his skin by thrusts of wit, paradox, common sense, and teasing symbolism, in preference to the preacher's tactic of frontal assault."[60] In fact, the very Hebrew word (*māšāl*, Proverbs 1:6) from which the

---

[58] Walter and Trudy Fremont. *Becoming an Effective Christian Counselor: A Practical Guide for Helping People* (Greenville, S.C.: Bob Jones University Press, 1996), 89.

[59] John Calvin, *Romans*, electronic ed., Calvin's Commentaries (Albany, Ore.: Ages Software, 1998), Ro 1:20.

[60] Kidner, *Proverbs*, 58-59.

book was named carries with it the idea of "illumination or comparison."[61]

Proverbs and parables are important elements of biblical teaching since all of

God's creation points man toward him. Solomon's use of riddles and parables to

teach his sons the importance of loving God was not original or exclusive to him

but was an important educational tool repeated throughout generations (Prov

4:4);[62] and described in Psalm 78:2-7:

> I will open my mouth in a parable; I will utter dark sayings from of old, things that we have heard and known, that our fathers have told us. We will not hide them from their children, but tell to the coming generation the glorious deeds of the Lord, and his might, and the wonders that he has done. He established a testimony in Jacob and appointed a law in Israel, which he commanded our fathers to teach to their children, that the next generation might know them, the children yet unborn, and arise and tell them to their children, *so that they should set their hope in God and not forget the works of God* [emphasis added], but keep his commandments.

This pattern of discipline is repeated throughout the Old Testament in passages

such as Deuteronomy 6:1-8[63] and Proverbs 6:21, 7:3.[64]

Like the Old Testament, the New Testament also uses parables, proverbs

and physical reminders of God's covenants, wisdom, works and character. One

---

[61] Derek Kidner, *Psalms 73–150: An Introduction and Commentary,* vol. 16 of Tyndale Old Testament Commentaries, ed. Donald J. Wiseman (Downers Grove: InterVarsity, 1975), 311.

[62] Proverbs 4:4 is often referred to as "the grandfather's lecture," since the father teaches his son what his father taught him. Many commentators see the father in these verses to be Solomon (Steveson, 58; Adams, *CCC Proverbs*, 39).

[63] Longman views Deuteronomy 6, Psalm 78:5-8, and Proverbs 4:4 as all showing how Jewish parents used illustrations/metaphors to pass down their religious traditions and teachings to the next generation (148).For further reading on the *Shema* and Jewish parental customs, see Craig Hartman, *Through Jewish Eyes* (Greenville, S.C.: Bob Jones University Press, 2010), 20-29.

[64] In speaking of the use of metaphors in Proverbs 7:3, Longman writes, "By such an admonition, the father is instructing the son that the command must change him internally (in the heart) and externally in terms of his actions (via the fingers)" (186). See also Waltke, *1-15,* 351.

example is found in 2 Timothy 2:1-7, where Paul uses various metaphors to offer counsel and wisdom.

> You then, *my child*, be strengthened by the grace that is in Christ Jesus, and what you have heard from me in the presence of many witnesses entrust to faithful men who will be able to teach others also. Share in suffering as a *good soldier* of Christ. No soldier gets entangled in civilian pursuits, since his aim is to please the one who enlisted him. *An athlete* is not crowned unless he competes according to the rules. It is the *hard-working farmer* who ought to have the first share of the crops. Think over what I say, for the Lord will give you understanding in everything (2 Tim 2:1-7, emphasis added).

Similarly, Christ is the perfect example of teaching with parables: "All these things Jesus said to the crowds in parables; indeed, he said nothing to them without a parable. This was to fulfill what was spoken by the prophet: 'I will open my mouth in parables; I will utter what has been hidden since the foundation of the world'" (Matt 13:34-35). Christ used dozens of parables in his teachings to give his disciples understanding of his special revelation (Matt 13:10-17).

Throughout the Old and the New Testaments, physical object lessons remind God's people of his character, his covenants, and his works. In Joshua 24:24-27, Israel erected a stone to remind the people of their covenant with God, and to this day a rainbow is a reminder that God is just, longsuffering, merciful, and faithful to his promises. Likewise, the Lord's Supper uses symbolic physical elements to help believers remember Christ's suffering, sacrifice, and love for his people (1 Cor 11:20-34). God knew that the natural tendency of people would be to forget valuable teaching and to be drawn away by misplaced desires, so he provided man with visual aids to remind him of Christ's preeminence. Proverbs 22:19-21 provides three reasons for the "dark sayings of counsel and knowledge": that "man's trust may be in the Lord," that man might "make known what is right and true," and that man may "give a true answer to those

110

who sent him." Proverbs, parables, and all physical realities when used to illuminate eternal truths increase faith in God's wisdom while also providing the hearer with discernment. This method of teaching becomes more important to parents whose child, in part because of his forgetfulness, has been given the ADHD label.[65]

The Rod of Correction

In addition to promoting the use of metaphors and examples to teach, Scripture also advocates instilling discipline by the use of the rod. However controversial corporal punishment may be,[66] Scripture states that the rod of correction[67] is essential to both teaching and correcting children in God's wisdom (Prov 22:15; 23:13-14). Concerning Proverbs 22:15, Waltke writes:

> *Folly*, not purity, *is bound up* [see 3:3; Gen 44:30] *in the heart* [see 2:11] *of youth* (see 1:4; 22:6). *The rod* [see 22:8] *of discipline* (*musar*; see 1:2) *will remove it far* [see 19:7] *from him* (see 22:5, 6). Youth's intractable insolence and his immoral propensity for laziness (13), lust (14), and greed (16) are tightly bound within his very constitution (15a; cf. Gen 8:21; Job

---

[65] Rachel Ehmke, "Helping Kids Who Struggle with Executive Function: Learning Specialists Discuss How to Get Organized"; available from http://www.childmind.org/en/posts/articles/2012-8-20-helping-kids-executive-functions-organization; Internet; accessed 26 March 2014. The therapist gives an example of using something familiar like a hamburger to teach a child something unfamiliar such as writing. She also points out that this method of teaching provides the student an object of familiarity to remember the associated lesson. The book of Proverbs utilizes similar methods using things like ants, ships, and treasure to help the reader understand and remember important truths. Parents can take field trips for the purpose of using God's natural creation to teach and ingrain eternal truth into the minds of their children. Similarly, something as simple as a flannel graph used to teach children can bring to mind Bible stories and associated truths even decades later.

[66] Edward M. Hallowell and John J. Ratey, *Driven to Distraction: Recognizing and Coping with Attention Deficit Disorder* (New York: Pantheon Books, 1994), 272.

[67] The physical act of spanking is set forth in the book of Proverbs as characteristic of wise parental discipline since it illuminates various spiritual realities. The New Testament does not mention this topic specifically as it relates to the father/son relationship and assumes that this wise parental practice should continue.

14:4; 25:4; Ps 51:5[7]; Isa 48:8), but the father's disciplining rod breaks folly's hold and frees him (v 15b).[68]

The rod of correction, paired with verbal reproof (Prov 29:15), is part of God's plan for parental discipleship.[69]

One way to understand the value of applying the rod and distinguish its use from violence is by comparing it to the vaccination process. This process is a clear illustration that a temporary sting can prevent death.[70] This comparison conveys God's intent for the parents' application of the rod to be for the loving purpose of protection and prevention. Loving parents would not think of holding their child down while another stabs the child in the leg with fine metal tubes that inject him with chemicals, yet most parents realize that a little pain applied by a physician can potentially prevent diseases and save a child from more severe pain and suffering, and even from death.

Much like the theory of vaccines, the application of the rod, as described by Scripture, inflicts a sting in order to produce spiritual life and health that will save the child from the pain of condemnation (Prov 23:13-14). Parents who love their children (Prov 13:24) use this physical aspect of biblical discipline to teach their children vital truths that guide them to the Savior. Spanking is not intended

---

[68] Waltke, *15-31*, 215-16.

[69] Ibid., 442-43.The Jewish commentator, Cohen, writes about Proverbs 29:15: "*Foolishness.* The Hebrew refers to delinquency which is here said to be *bound up* in a child, i.e., a natural state in the early period of life. Toy aptly quotes a saying of Menander, a Greek poet of the fourth century, 'He who is not flogged is not educated'" (148). Additionally, McKane writes, "Verses 15 and 17 are also concerned with matter of parental discipline and represent that corporal punishment is an indispensable element of discipline and education" (634).

[70] This illustration is not intended to encourage or discourage vaccinating children. It is merely an example.

to be violent, abusive, or destructive,[71] but to gently and lovingly teach wisdom that will lead the child to the Savior (Prov 22:15; 29:15). This application of discipline speaks directly to the senses of the child and demands he pay attention.

The Benefits of Athletics

Physical exercise is another illustration employed throughout Scripture to teach the value of personal discipline. Likewise, parents can use exercise and athletics to teach their children as well. The child who participates in organized physical activities stands to receive not only tremendous physical benefits but also the opportunity to learn transforming spiritual lessons.[72] Godly parents and Christian coaches can use the platform of athletics to build relationships and to teach children both about staying focused and about making immediate sacrifices to achieve goals (1 Cor 9:24-25; Phil 2:16). Children can also benefit from learning to ignore distractions and eliminate bad habits (Heb 12:1-2), to prepare diligently (1 Pet 1:13-14), to obey standardized rules and follow directions (2 Tim 2:5), to complete the course through endurance (Phil 3:14; Heb 12:1), and to learn physical and mental control (1 Cor 9:24-27).

---

[71] John MacArthur, "Parenting in an Anti-Spanking Culture"; available from http://www.gty.org/Resources/articles/3127; Internet; accessed 7 December 2012.

[72] It is important to note though, that athletics is not a cure to the child's genuine problems, and sports can even be detrimental to a child without proper guidance and right teaching from a Christian worldview.

Children who are hyperactive, who have trouble listening, who are disobedient, who have trouble sleeping,[73] or who have little self-control usually benefit from participation in organized athletics.[74] Michael Phelps, American swimmer and the most decorated Olympian of all time, is one example of someone who, as a child, was diagnosed with ADHD but whose behavior, bodily-control, and attention span improved when he began participating in competitive swimming: "Ms. Phelps watched the boy who couldn't sit still at school sit for four hours at a meet waiting to swim his five minutes' worth of races."[75] Athletics and structured exercise provide the high-energy child with an outlet to burn off some energy which can positively affect his life. Though most educational systems currently demand that children sit still for lengthy periods, children often have a physical need for motion as relates to their developmental age.[76] Physical exercise and organized athletics, when biblically applied, can not

---

[73] Madeline Vann, "The Best Sports for Children with ADHD"; available from http://www.everydayhealth.com/adhd/best-sports-for-children-with-adhd.aspx; Internet. Though written from a secular standpoint, the article points out the many benefits that sports provide children, a fact which has led some doctors to prescribe participation in organized sports as part of their therapy. The article states, "Behavior of children with ADHD can improve with at least 40 minutes of activity a day. Some families report that sports help their children with ADHD sleep better and have fewer outbursts or meltdowns."

[74] Patty Neighmond, "Exercise Helps Students in the Classroom"; available from http://www.npr.org/templates/story/story.php?storyId=5742152; Internet.

[75] Michael Winerip, "Phelps's Mother Recalls Helping Her Son Find Gold-Medal Focus"; available from http://www.nytimes.com/2008/08/10/sports/olympics/10Rparent.html?pagewanted=all&_r=0; Internet.

[76] National Institute of Health, "Exercise for Children"; available from http://www.nlm.nih.gov/medlineplus/exerciseforchildren.html; Internet; accessed 4 January 2014.

only serve as tangible illustrations of sanctification, but they also promote a physically healthy and well-balanced child.[77]

Though athletics and exercise can be beneficial, not all children are physically capable of participating. Numerous other forms of physical disciplines are also available for believing parents to engage their children. The fields of music, art, auto-mechanics, and others offer children a platform for physical and mental self-control similar to athletics which parents can use to teach biblical lessons and cultivate godly character.

Scriptural Theology – Proverbs 3:5-35

In addition to presenting right patterns and clear illustrations, parents who are committed to discipling their children must verbally teach sound theology in a way that encourages their children's spiritual health in Christ:[78] "The wise of heart makes his speech judicious and adds persuasiveness to his lips. [His] gracious words are like a honeycomb, sweetness to the soul and health to the body" (Prov 16:22-24).[79] Proverbs 3 in particular is helpful in teaching scriptural theology in order to direct children toward a right relationship with Christ; it teaches God's trustworthiness (5-8), preeminence (9-10), loving-

---

[77] American Academy of Pediatrics, "Organized Sports for Children and Preadolescents"; available from http://pediatrics.aappublications.org/content/107/6/1459.full; Internet; accessed 5 January 2013.

[78] For further reading on using Scripture to disciple children, see Lou Priolo, *Teach Them Diligently: How to Use the Scriptures in Child Training*.

[79] Literally, the wise man's speech encourages others to learn what comes out of his mouth (wisdom) (Steveson, 223). Waltke writes, "Those who possess prudence become a life-giving spring that is so attractive that they 'turn away' the community from folly to drink from their teachings (see 10:11; 13:14: 14:27)" (*15-31*, 29).

kindness (11-12), promises (16-18), sovereignty (19-20), deliverance (21-35), and righteousness (32-35).

God's Promises

Biblical theology is vital to families with a child who has been given the ADHD label, and God's promises (Prov 3:16-18) and covenants are a good example[80] of how practical Scripture is. Though the secular concept of behavior modification must be rejected as manipulative, the practice of offering rewards and negative consequences is, in truth, a biblical concept that therapists have altered to fit their secular theories.[81] In contrast to behavior modification that focuses on outward change,[82] God's promises encourage holiness (inward change that produces outward change) based on a loving and righteous relationship with God.[83] For example, Paul states, "Since we have these promises, beloved, let us cleanse ourselves from every defilement of body and spirit, bringing holiness to completion in the fear of God" (2 Cor 7:1).[84] To state it

---

[80] These promises in Proverbs 3 pertain to the blessings or results of acquiring divine wisdom (Kidner, *Proverbs*, 65).

[81] Adams, *The Christian Counselor's Manual*, 164-70.

[82] Wender, *ADHD*, 102-10.

[83] For further reading on the process of sanctification, see Bryan Chapell, *Holiness by Grace: Delighting in the Joy That Is Our Strength* (Wheaton: Crossway, 2001).

[84] Regarding the promises: "The promises referred to are, first, the indwelling of God (6:16); second, his favor (verse 17); third, that they would be his sons and daughters (verse 18). **Therefore** (KJV), says the apostle, having these promises of intimate association with God and this assurance of his love, **let us purify ourselves**" (Charles Hodge, *2 Corinthians*, vol. 12 of Crossway Classic Commentaries, ed. Alister McGrath and J. I. Packer (Wheaton: Crossway, 1995), 2 Co 7:1). See also Colin G. Kruse, *2 Corinthians: An Introduction and Commentary*, vol. 8 of Tyndale New Testament Commentaries (Downers Grove: InterVarsity, 1987).

more bluntly, salvation is centered on a covenant promise from God the father. Our entire relationship with God is based on this reality by faith.

In the same manner, Proverbs 3 gives several desirable consequences for those who pursue wisdom and a relationship with God: length of days (2, 16), peace (2, 17), grace (4, 34), right relationships (4), security (6, 23, 26), physical health (8), provisions (10, 16), holiness (14, 24), honor (16, 22, 35), pleasant life (17), eternal life (18, 22), happiness (18), mental stability (24, 25), and a joyful home (33). On the other hand, Solomon also records negative consequences for those who choose their own way above God: a cursed house (33), rejection and separation from God (34), and a dishonorable life (35). God's promises and warnings are intended to restore man both inwardly and, consequently, behaviorally to the image of God (2 Pet 1:3-11).

Though parents must follow God's example by providing clear rules, promises, warnings, and consequences, these things are useless and may even be detrimental to a child if they do not direct the child toward the desired goal of faith in God and growth in holiness. Discipline without clearly established goals is not discipline at all. Too many parents and teachers punish children for wrong behavior or decisions instead of disciplining them toward the proper goals. Correction and instruction are both part of discipline, but these differ greatly from punishment. True biblical authoritative discipline that is patterned after God's discipline is centered on a worthy goal (Hebrews 12:1-13 is one example). This truth is why reproof, rebuke, correction and instruction are all necessary aspects of discipline, and why punishment does not lead anyone toward a goal.

God never punishes those he loves, since he took our punishment.[85] He does, however discipline all those whom he loves (Hebrews 12:5ff.).

Since discipline is moving the child from point A (his naturally foolish condition) toward point B (becoming wise), rules and regulations help keep the child focused on the goal. Some parental rules and consequences may seem to be biblical, yet rules and consequences without proper biblical teaching can foster a legalistic mindset that fails to motivate children toward an intimate relationship with the Lord; this relationship is the ultimate goal. Other parents encourage worldliness and self-destruction by ignoring or refusing to have rules, rewards, and negative consequences. In essence, they have not established God's goal for their child. Still others make promises and warnings yet fail to follow through, and thus they may provoke their children to anger and discouragement. Wise parents think through their rules, rewards, consequences, and regulations in order to guide children toward the goal of covenant holiness. It is worth noting, however, that the law or rules are merely a tutor that leads the child toward the goal. This reality is true of God's law over his children and must be true with an earthly father's rules and regulations with his children.

Additionally, when parents provide and uphold clear promises and warnings, the child learns to consider future rewards and consequences and to exercise self-control. This teaching process is especially relevant to those children who are diagnosed with ADHD, since secularists suggest that these children are

---

[85] Bryan Chapell devotes an entire chapter in his book *Holiness by Grace: Delighting in the Joy That Is Our Strength* to revealing that God's discipline is never punishment but is entirely His grace. (Wheaton: Crossway, 2001).

unable to regulate "long-term self-interest"[86] and incapable of self-control.[87]
Barkley explains, "For self-control to occur, the individual must have developed
a preference for the long-term over the short-term outcomes of behavior."[88] In
other words, his widely held hypothesis views the child diagnosed with ADHD
to have a biological defect in his neurological system that "inhibits" foreseeing
future reward over immediate gratification, and therefore the ADHD child is
unable to maintain self-control.[89] In reality, this hypothesis has no scientific
proof, and other than the alleged physical "inhibitors," the hypothesis describes
almost all children and many adults. Many people, especially children, have
trouble trusting in things that are unseen or delayed, and part of the learning
process that every individual must go through is to be taught the value of living
in light of the future and not merely for immediate gratification.

Furthermore, motivation is required to accomplish any worthy goal, and
likewise, self-control must be present. Scripture teaches that self-control is a fruit
of the Spirit (Gal 5:23) and that it is cultivated through faith in God as well as
through attentiveness and submission to God's Word. Without the faithful and
loving promises of God and the right goal to please him, parents can never
expect a child to have self-control for the purpose of pleasing God (1 Tim 4:7-8),[90]

---

[86] NoSC, 302.

[87] Ibid., 64.

[88] Ibid., 52.

[89] Ibid., 46.

[90] "Discipline is from *gumnazō*, from which our English words 'gymnasium' and
'gymnastics' derive. It means 'to train,' or 'to exercise.' The word speaks of the rigorous,
strenuous, self-sacrificing training an athlete undergoes. Every Greek city had its gymnasium,
and Ephesus was no exception. Youths customarily spent much of their time from ages sixteen to
eighteen in physical training. That was vital, since life in those days involved much physical

let alone a mindset of faith that is focused on eternity. Too many parents and teachers are dependent upon medication to provide self-control in their children rather than depending upon the Holy Spirit to cultivate fruit in the hearts of those He loves. In many Christian's lives, medication has become an acceptable substitute for the work of the Holy Spirit, yet pharmaceutics can never change the heart and draw men unto the Lord.

God's Deliverance

Another theological concept that is crucial in discipline and more so with a child diagnosed with ADHD is that there is hope because God offers deliverance to those who receive his wisdom (Prov 3:21-35). Proverbs 3 lists some specific things from which God's wisdom delivers man: insecurity and anxiety (23, 25), fear and insomnia (24), and sin (26). Likewise, God's wisdom saves man from his self-centeredness (27), his natural tendency to withhold justice (28), his violent heart (29-31), and his tendency to envy others even in wickedness (31). These emotions, mindsets, and behaviors are often labeled as "psychiatric disorders" or criteria of disorders[91] by secularists, yet God declares these sins to be the products of a heart that is "devious" (32), "wicked" (33), "scornful" (34),

---

activity. There was a great emphasis on physical training and the glory of winning athletic events. By using *gumnazō*, Paul plays off that cultural phenomenon and applies it to the spiritual realm. As Greek culture emphasized dedicated training of the body, Paul urged Timothy to discipline himself for the purpose of godliness. The present tense of the verb indicates that was to be Timothy's constant pursuit. Timothy was to train his inner man for godliness" (John F. MacArthur Jr., *1 Timothy*, MacArthur New Testament Commentary [Chicago: Moody, 1995], 163). See also Mounce, *Pastoral Epistles*, 250–51.

[91] Wender, *ADHD*, 255-57.

"foolish" (35), and in need of God's deliverance. Children may not yet be considered devious, wicked, or scornful, but their hearts are filled with the same foolishness that can lead them to be characterized in this fashion. God, however, is able to deliver the most difficult and sinful people from their depraved nature and from their worst behaviors.

Conclusion

Though it may seem that a child labelled as ADHD's most pressing needs are behavioral, his or her greatest needs are actually spiritual, so the real agent of change will be the Holy Spirit. Parents, however, are responsible and must endeavor to remove barriers to spiritual regeneration and restoration. Counselors, teachers, and parents, as fellow recipients of God's grace, must clearly communicate the hope found in the unchanging truth of Scripture and the abundant riches of Christ, which can meet the needs of a troubled heart. Without the grace of God, the working of the Holy Spirit, and the supreme example of Christ as the focus of the parent/child relationship, there is no genuine remedy. Effective discipline or discipleship, then, must be theocentric if it is to meet the child's greatest needs.

CONCLUSION

The continued increase in ADHD diagnoses in American reveals an alarming problem, especially since secularists still admit that they have not discovered what causes their idea of ADHD, nor do they yet know the valid remedy to address a child's maladaptive behaviors. This failure results from secular beliefs that dismiss God's Word as the best source to understand the nature of man, as well as his behavior, his spiritual nature, and his relationship to God. For decades, parents, who are best positioned by God to help children, have, in general, blindly accepted secular theories, which at their core, claim that the child's behavioral problems are medical and not something that a parent should attempt to address. After careful objective study, however, it is clear that parents are uniquely qualified by God to discipline their children. Not only can parents offer the only valid remedy that addresses the whole child and provides hope for right change, but Scripture gives parents the responsibility to do so.

Furthermore, Scripture equips families with right understanding of both behavior in general and specific behaviors. As previously stated, not all behaviors listed in the *DSM* are sinful, yet Scripture deals with each behavior in some way or another. The Bible does determine many of these behaviors to be sinful or rooted in man's sinful nature, and the wise will always agree with these immutable judgments rather than with secular theories and constructs on specific behaviors or groups of behaviors. The sinful patterns of behavior

exhibited in children diagnosed as ADHD are normal products of a depraved

heart, since Scripture proclaims that all have sinned and that no temptation to sin

exists that is not a common human experience (1 Cor 10:13).[1] All sins, no matter

how someone may try to categorize them, group them with other sins, or rename

them, are normal activity for the heart pursuing its own way and giving into

temptation. Though all children pursue different desires and give in to different

sins (Jas 1:14-15),[2] the normal way of thinking sees no reason to pursue glorifying

God, and in fact, without saving faith, the unregenerate heart cannot please God

(Heb 11:6).[3] This pattern of giving in to sin will continue until sin fully controls

[1] "But here it is used in a broad sense which includes both 'test' and 'temptation'. Nothing exceptional in either way had happened to the Corinthians. They had experienced only *what is common to man*. And God is not simply a spectator of the affairs of life; he is concerned and active. Believers can count on his help. He will always make *a way out*" (Leon Morris, *First Epistle of Paul to the Corinthians*, vol. 7 of Tyndale New Testament Commentaries [Downers Grove: InterVarsity, 1985], 142). See also Charles Hodge, *1 Corinthians*, vol. 11 of Crossway Classic Commentaries, ed. Alister McGrath and J. I. Packer (Wheaton: Crossway, 1995), 170-71.

[2] Moo writes, "If he wants to blame someone, he has only himself to consider — temptation comes from *his own desire*. *Desire* (*epithymia*) does not always have a bad meaning (cf. Luke 22:15; Phil. 1:23), but here, as most often in the New Testament, it refers to fleshly, selfish, illicit desire. While the word often describes specifically sexual passions, the use of the singular here suggests a broader conception. Like the rabbis, who spoke of 'the evil impulse' (*yeser hara*) that inhabits every person, James seems to think of man's innate tendency towards sin. Temptation springs from this 'evil impulse', as it *lures* and *entices* man" (Douglas J. Moo, *James: An Introduction and Commentary*, vol. 16 of Tyndale New Testament Commentaries [Downers Grove: InterVarsity, 1985], 75–76). See also Thomas Manton, *James*. Crossway Classic Commentaries, ed. Alister McGrath and J. I. Packer (Wheaton: Crossway, 1995), 59.

[3] "The life that pleases God begins with the certain recognition of God and his character. This is stated explicitly in the explanatory clause that follows immediately, which clarifies two rudimentary dimensions of πίστις, 'faith.' The only presupposition for approaching God is the certainty that he exists and that he establishes a relationship with those who earnestly seek him" (William L. Lane, *Hebrews 9–13*, vol. 47B of Word Biblical Commentary [Dallas: Word, 1998], 337–38). "But he is arguing from man's experience of communion with God to the fact that his faith in God's existence must be real. (ii) Such worshippers must also believe *that he rewards those who seek him*. This statement is intended to reassure those who are questioning whether the quest for God is always successful. It needs faith to accept this, but the conviction that God rewards the serious seeker is fully in harmony with the nature of God as he has made himself known throughout his revelations to men. There is no fear that any seeker may not find him if he acts in faith" (Donald

his life. For the believer, however, Scripture provides hope for man's inability to please God and deliverance from his destructive and controlling behaviors and mindsets. First Corinthians 10:13 states that with God's faithful help, we can overcome every temptation:[4] "God is faithful, and will not let you be tempted beyond your ability, but with the temptation he will also provide the way of escape, that you may be able to endure it." This reality undermines the widely accepted secular theory that claims children diagnosed as ADHD have a genetic or physical inability to say no to sinful behavior. Instead of viewing a child's bad behaviors as indicative of a disease that impairs his ability to act normally, parents must accept the biblical view that reveals their child's bad behaviors to be evidence of the common sin nature that prevents him from pleasing God. He or she is not abnormal. Without Christ, the unregenerate heart will always act in a depraved manner. The Holy Spirit, however, enables believers to obey him (Rom 8:4-11),[5] and Christ provides us the power to make it through life's difficult circumstances (Phil 4:13) — the behaviors listed in the *DSM* as indicators of ADHD are no exception. This wonderful hope and sure remedy is truth that parents must embrace and offer to their children.

Though the secular label may initially obscure the heart conditions that produce most of the behaviors characteristic of the ADHD label and even

---

Guthrie, *Hebrews: An Introduction and Commentary*, vol. 15 of Tyndale New Testament Commentaries [Downers Grove: InterVarsity, 1983], 232).

[4] Hodge, *1 Corinthians*, 171.

[5] F. F. Bruce, *Romans: An Introduction and Commentary*, vol. 6 of Tyndale New Testament Commentaries (Downers Grove: InterVarsity, 1985), 163–66; Charles Hodge, *Romans*, Crossway Classic Commentaries, ed. Alister McGrath and J. I. Packer (Wheaton: Crossway, 1993), Ro 8:4–7.

suggest that a child might be mentally ill, the real problem and its solution have existed since the fall of Adam. In fact, Scripture assumes that the naturally depraved heart of every child apart from grace will produce destructive behaviors which are self-focused, carnal, and oppositional to both God and man. While behaviors and circumstances may vary among children, those whom secularists have diagnosed as ADHD are not abnormal or mentally ill but are in need of changed hearts through the transforming work of the Holy Spirit. It is divine wisdom that alone can deliver a child from his depraved nature. Cohen writes, "As [wisdom] then changed chaos to order, so it can affect each human life (19-20)."[6] Parents who possess God's wisdom and desire God to change the chaos in the heart of a child must offer that child a covenant relationship with God and allow the Holy Spirit to transform the child's life. It is time that we embrace the truth of the gospel and graciously dismiss the ADHD label for what it is: an unscientific, unreliable, and outright misleading construct. We must promote the truth of the gospel in order to sincerely love our children and provide them with genuine hope and valid biblical answers.

---

[6] Abraham Cohen, *Proverbs* (London: Soncino Press, 1973), 17.

APPENDICES

APPENDIX A – THE PROVERBIAL FOOL

Since one of the most important discussions surrounding ADHD is anthropology, it is necessary to carefully examine some of the key biblical terms in Proverbs that directly relate to the child's heart and behaviors. Specifically, one needs to understand man's position before God in relation to divine wisdom. By extension such a definition should include discussion on who can receive God's wisdom. While the term *biblical fool* can refer to one who has a hardened heart, which is set against God, the term is also used to describe the natural hearts of all unregenerate people without understanding of divine wisdom.[1]

General Description

Scripture states that a fool is anyone who trusts in his own mind over God's wisdom.[2] For example, Proverbs 28:26 states this important definition: "Whoever trusts in his own mind is a fool, but he who walks in wisdom will be

---

[1] Bruce Waltke, *The Book of Proverbs: Chapters 1-15*, New International Commentary on the Old Testament, ed. R. K. Harrison and Robert L. Hubbard Jr. (Grand Rapids: Eerdmans, 2004), 93-94; Derek Kidner, *Proverbs: An Introduction and Commentary*, Tyndale Old Testament Commentaries, ed. Donald J. Wiseman (Downers Grove: InterVarsity, 1977), 39-42

[2] Longman points out that "to trust in one's own heart is the epitome of folly because the heart is limited in its knowledge and also, apart from a relationship with God, wicked" (Tremper Longman III, *Proverbs*, Baker Commentary on the Old Testament Wisdom and Psalms [Grand Rapids: Baker, 2006], 496-97).

delivered."[3] Waltke points out that the word *fool* is often used in Proverbs "as a standard of comparison for one who is wise in his own eyes."[4] He also notes that this verse implies the depravity of the human heart and its need for divine wisdom.[5] Based on this understanding, everyone without God's wisdom is naturally a fool.[6] It is no wonder that Proverbs 22:15 declares that foolishness is bound in the heart of every child, since the natural bent of every child is to trust in his own mind.[7] Proverbs 22:15 has even been called "the doctrine of 'original

---

[3] Cohen writes that the fool is one who "neglects the principles of wisdom and follows his own judgment" (Abraham Cohen, *Proverbs* [London: Soncino Press, 1973], 192). Likewise, Longman comments: "To trust in one's own heart (note the linkage by contrast to the second colon of the previous proverb) is the epitome of folly because the heart is limited in its knowledge an also, apart from relationship with God, wicked" (Longman, 496-97). Wiersbe sees the comparison between the fool's pride and Satan's lie to mankind in the Garden of Eden: "You will be like God (Gen 3:5; *NKJV*)" Warren W. Wiersbe, *Be Skillful: Tapping God's Guidebook to Fulfillment* (Wheaton: Victor Books, 1995), 77.

[4] Waltke, *1-15*, 50.

[5] Waltke, *15-31*, 427.

[6] Kidner writes, "The fact the fool, by whatever name he goes, is by definition one whose mind is closed, for the present, at least, to God (like the *nabal* of Psa 14:1) and to reason (like the *Nabal* of whom of whom his wife said, 'One cannot speak to him', 1 Sam 25:17), since he has rejected the first principle of wisdom, the fear of the Lord" (*Proverbs*, 41).

[7] Longman comments on Proverbs 22:15 that "the first colon states the sorry condition of youth, and the second gives the prescription for rectifying the problem. . . . The 'heart,' roughly equivalent to what we would call character, of the young is bad. The term 'stupidity' is closely associated with folly. It takes the application of discipline to remove their stupidity, which is so integrally and naturally a part of a person" (408). Whereas Proverbs 22:15 focuses on the foolishness of the natural heart of every child and the necessary remedy being the rod of discipline, Proverbs 29:15 states that wisdom, the antithesis of foolishness, is the benefit of discipline. Whybray writes that when a child is "freed from proper discipline" he will shame his mother (R. N. Whybray, *Proverbs*, New Century Bible Commentary [Grand Rapids: Eerdmans, 1994], 402). Motivating a foolish child to receive wisdom requires verbal teaching but also physical instruction (William McKane, *Proverbs: A New Approach* [Philadelphia: Westminster, 1970], 565). See also Cohen, 148.

folly.'"[8] Though born foolish, the one who walks in God's wisdom will be delivered (Proverbs 28:26).[9] Although the context of Proverbs would indicate that deliverance in verse 26 is general in nature (from danger, social problems, and even death), Longman has the New Testament perspective in mind and sees this passage as also explaining future salvation that Christ would accomplish.[10] Both in temporal and eternal applications, God's wisdom is the antithesis of the fool/self-reliance.[11] Proverbs 3:5-6 also states a similar idea, contrasting self-trust with whole-hearted trust in the Lord through intimate relationship with him.[12] The common characteristics of all three types of biblical fools are that they live in

---

[8] Whybray, 125; Adams also sees Proverbs 22:15 as revealing man's depraved nature: "The doctrine of original sin is taught in verse 15. The bent of the heart is in the wrong direction" (CCC Proverbs, 174).

[9] Jay Adams comments on this verse in reference to biblical counseling: "Wisdom from God, found in His Word, is what men need [in counseling]; not their own ideas (cf. Isaiah 55:6-11). There could hardly be a more anti-Rogerian statement than that found in this verse. Divine wisdom alone (not one's own heart) can point out the safe road in life or in death" (The Christian Counselor's Commentary: Proverbs [Woodruff, S.C.: Timeless Texts, 1997], 214); (hereafter referred to as Adams, CCC Proverbs). Longman notes that the walking of the wise is in keeping with the proverbial metaphor of the way. In light of New Testament truths, one can see the idea of progressive sanctification as the disciple, who has received wisdom, walks with Christ, who is wisdom (497).

[10] Longman, 497; Waltke sees the deliverance of the wise referring to the Lord's punishment of fools (1:32-33; 2:20-22) (15-31, 427-28).

[11] "Wisdom entails fear of Yahweh (1:7) and an aversion to self-reliance (3:5, 7; 26:12; 27:1; 28:11)" (Longman, 497).

[12] The prepositional phrases "unto Yahweh" and "unto your own discernment" are antithetical, or as Phillips points out, "They are two rival ways of thinking, two antagonists. The one leaves me locked into my own inborn foolishness and waywardness (Prov 12:15; 22:15; cf. Ps. 51:5). The other puts me in the way of God" (God's Wisdom in Proverbs: Hearing God's Voice in Scripture [The Woodlands, Tex: Kress Biblical Resources, 2011], 136); (Waltke, 15-31, 427). Kidner writes, "Acknowledge is quite simply 'know', which contains not only the idea of acknowledging, but the much richer content of being 'aware of', and having 'fellowship with'" (Proverbs, 63-64).

pursuit of their desires,[13] they lack divine wisdom,[14] they are headed toward destruction,[15] "they are characterized by lack of self-control" (Prov 12:16),[16] and they behave foolishly (by doing so they reflect the absence of God's wisdom in their lives; Prov 13:16).[17]

While Scripture considers all unsaved who are capable of understanding divine wisdom to be fools,[18] believers can also play the fool by trusting in their own minds and behaving accordingly. In Ephesians 5:17 Paul reveals this truth by giving the believer an imperative: "Therefore do not be foolish, but understand what the will of the Lord is [wisdom]."[19] Even those who possess

---

[13] Tedd Tripp, *Shepherding a Child's Heart* (Wapwallopen, Pa.: Shepherd Press, 1995), 106; Cohen, 6; Waltke, *1-15*, 202-4.

[14] See Kidner's discussion on *nabal* (*Proverbs*, 41); Waltke, *1-15*, 111-12; Paul points out in Titus 3:3 that prior to receiving Christ, all Christians were foolish (*anoetos*) or without understanding (Donald Guthrie, *Pastoral Epistles: An Introduction and Commentary*, vol. 14 of *Tyndale New Testament Commentaries* [Downers Grove: InterVarsity, 1990], 224); Cohen, 6.

[15] Longman, 497; Waltke, *15-31*, 428.

[16] Bruce Waltke, *The Book of Proverbs: Chapters 15-30*, New International Commentary on the Old Testament, ed. R. K. Harrison and Robert L. Hubbard Jr. (Grand Rapids: Eerdmans, 2005), 344; Kidner, *Proverbs*, 97; Cohen, 76.

[17] "*Paras*, glossed *spreads out* (*yipros*), takes as its objects a garment, fishing net, snare, and so on. Here it is used metaphorically with the particular sense of 'to display,' 'like a peddler who openly spreads his wares before the gaze of all men.' Its parallels are 'proclaims' (12:13) and 'gushes' (15:3). By its antithesis to 'take cover' ('to protect himself'), 'to spread out folly' entails that he ruins himself thereby. Among other things the fool shows his annoyance at once (12:16)" Waltke, *1-15*, 298, 566-67); Longman, 288-89.

[18] Waltke writes that "Proverbs divides humanity into two classes: the wise and righteous over against fools and the wicked. These wisdom and ethical terms are correlative, for though they do not mean the same thing, they have the same referent" (*1-15*, 93).

[19] Lincoln comments on Ephesians 5:17: "Those who have already been exhorted not to live as unwise people in v 15 are now again warned not to succumb to folly. . . . The contrast between wise and unwise is now replaced by that between being foolish and having understanding. Just as the children of light will learn what is pleasing to the Lord (5:10), so those who are wise will understand what the will of the Lord is. Indeed, understanding the will of the

God's wisdom can behave foolishly when they lack right desire to please the Lord and demonstrate in their behaviors that they are walking in the flesh.[20]

Specific Types

Although Proverbs uses the word *fool* in a general sense to describe all people who are able to accept divine wisdom yet have not received God's wisdom,[21] Proverbs also describes three specific types of fools:[22] (1) the simple, naïve, or "inexperienced" fool (Prov 14:15),[23] (2) the dull, stupid, or "ordinary fool"[24] (Prov 1:32; 26:11; 27:22),[25] and (3) the scornful, mocker, or "hardened" fool (Prov 1:22, 29; 3:34-35; 14:6-7; 19:29).[26] Waltke explains Proverbs' use of these names:

Lord is the heart of wisdom (cf. also Col 1:9, 'filled with the knowledge of his will in all spiritual wisdom and understanding'). For believers, wise living involves a practical perception dependent on the direction of their Lord" (Andrew T. Lincoln, *Ephesians*, vol. 42 of Word Biblical Commentary [Dallas: Word, 1990], 342-43).

[20] "'Do not be senseless, undiscriminating between what is true and false, right and wrong, important and unimportant, but understanding (i.e., discerning) what God's will is.' That is, see things as God sees them, and make his will or judgment your standard and the rule of your conduct" (Charles Hodge, *Ephesians*, vol. 7 of Crossway Classic Commentaries, ed. Alister McGrath and J. I. Packer [Wheaton: Crossway, 1994], 178).

[21] The book of Proverbs contains three different Hebrew words along with three different names to describe fools. Some commentators include a sluggard as potentially a fourth type of fool. For more reading on the three types of proverbial fools, see Waltke, *1-15*, 109-15 and Kidner, *Proverbs*, 39-42.

[22] Kidner, *Proverbs*, 39-41; Waltke, *1-15*, 93-94.

[23] Waltke, *15-31*, 252; Kidner, *Proverbs*, 39.

[24] Kidner, *Proverbs*, 42.

[25] Many theologians see the three Hebrew words *kesil*, *'ewil*, and *nabal* as best describing the ordinary fool, though they note that these "terms are virtually interchangeable" with the other names of the simple fool and the scorner (Ibid., 39-41); Waltke, *1-15*, 93-94.

[26] Kidner, *Proverbs*, 41-42, Waltke, *1-15*, 114.

These ethical terms imply the fool's moral culpability, not his lack of intelligence. The wisdom terms for the unwise, however, are not correlatives but distinguish three of four classes of fools according to their educative capacities: the gullible, the fool, and the mocker.[27]

As Waltke emphasizes, the determining factor for a fool is not his intellectual capabilities, but rather his lack of God's wisdom and trust in the fool's own understanding.[28]

General Applications

All children (and adults) who should understand and receive divine wisdom yet are without it are biblical fools: either being a simple fool, an ordinary fool, or a hardened fool (scorner). Biblical understanding of the fool is important in order for biblical parental discipline to occur. Specifically, having this understanding helps parents discern the current direction of the child diagnosed with ADHD through both his reactions to God's wisdom as well his behaviors, which can reveal the position of his foolish heart.

Understanding Rather Than Labelling

Although, a child may be a type of proverbial fool and engage in foolish behaviors, it is wise to refrain from using the term *fool* or one of the specific names (such as, gullible or scorner) to describe your child since doing so could easily confuse or even anger him or her.[29] Proverbs utilizes the names and words

---

[27] Waltke, *1-15*, 111.

[28] Cohen likewise notes that fools are not intellectually stupid: "They are morally, rather than intellectually, defective, and despise a father's correction" (3).

[29] Merriam-Webster's dictionary offers four definitions including: "A harmlessly deranged person or one lacking in common powers of understanding" (s. v. "fool," available from http://www.merriam-webster.com/dictionary/fool; Internet; accessed 14 April 2014). Such definitions differ from the biblical idea of a fool and are commonly thought of when the word is used.

for fool to provide understanding to the reader and warn the child against ignoring or refusing divine wisdom.[30] In other words, these terms help the reader to know where a heart is in relationship to God and his wisdom and thus to understand his current direction in life and his projected destination as well as to gain practical advice on how to better educate him. This understanding of the proverbial fool also provides parents and children warning against these types of dangerous and destructive hearts.

Along the same lines, the theological metaphor of a path or way found throughout the book of Proverbs suggests that the designations of wise and foolish represent the two options one has in life.[31] A person can choose the way of wisdom/life (progressing in sanctification) or choose the way of folly/death (progressively moving away from divine wisdom).[32] There exists no moral neutrality. This metaphor emphasizes the idea that the term is more than a label: it denotes direction and ultimately destination.[33] People are always moving further away from God — going from being a simple fool to an ordinary fool to a

---

[30] Waltke writes concerning the book of Proverbs preamble that it "was written for parents and teachers who will use the book, articulates the book's aim (1:2-6) and its addressees, namely, Israel's educable youth (4-5)." The preamble, coupled with the prologue and title, leads Waltke to conclude that the book is written to know wisdom and to understand its expression (1-15, 174). Wiersbe likewise states the purpose of Proverbs to be relational: "Solomon's aim in writing this book is to help us become skillful in relating to both people and circumstances so that we can make a success out of life to the glory of God" (Warren Wiersbe, *Be Skillful: Tapping God's Guidebook to Fulfillment* [Wheaton: Victor Books, 1995], 61). Therefore, the purpose of God's revealing various types of fools is not for the reader to cast everyone into groups, but rather to understand wisdom that can be applied in varied relationships.

[31] Longman, 300, 497; Kidner, *Proverbs*, 54-56.

[32] Kidner, *Proverbs*, 55-56; "One must decide between wisdom begotten by God and folly that stands as wisdom's rival" (Waltke, *1-15*, 125).

[33] Kidner, *Proverbs*, 54-56

hardened fool—or they are drawing closer to him through wisdom. Therefore, rather than calling children by these terms, parents can use their understanding of these classifications to best approach the child and instruct him toward divine wisdom.

God's Counsel Rather Than Man's

Scripture also offers insight into how parents should wisely educate their children. Proverbs 22:6, when understood within the whole context of Proverbs, which is centered on the education of divine wisdom, reveals the parents' responsibility not only to discern their child's natural bent, but also to dedicate/train that child toward the right way. In other words, parents are first responsible to direct the child's life. Waltke emphasizes that the *dedication* of the child to *his way* implies that the child is young and still pliable/teachable.[34] Parents are to dedicate their child "according to his (the child's) way,"[35] or according to the physical and mental abilities of the developing youth."[36] Waltke notes, however, that the child's natural way, no matter how unique the child might be, is foolish.[37] Therefore parents must dedicate or wisely decide to approach the child where he is at in reference to wisdom and his ability to understand. Similarly, McKane states,

> 'According to his way' does not mean 'according to the way he ought to go'. The thought that the educational process must be tailored to the requirements of the individual is not

---

[34] Waltke, *15-31*, 204; Kidner, *Proverbs*, 37.

[35] Kidner, *Proverbs*, 147.

[36] Waltke, *15-31*, 204-5.

[37] Waltke points out, "The other six references to *na'ar* univocally characterize his way as foolish" (ibid., 205).

at all what is intended. There is only one right way — the way of life — and the educational discipline which directs young men along this way is uniform.[38]

This principle truth assumes, of course, that children are better able to

understand divine wisdom as they mature. Nonetheless, instruction should

begin at an early age.[39] Waltke states: "In sum, the proverb implies that the

religious and moral initiation of the youth should be oriented from the first to

counteract his foolish way."[40] McKane also writes, "The importance of education

for the young is also stressed in verse 6. This is the age when impressionability

can be taken for granted and when change for the better is possible."[41] If parents

see at an early age that children have specific foolish traits bound up within their

hearts as observed in their actions (e.g., they are more resistant to listening to

their authority, are lazy, or are loud and boisterous), then they should recognize

these behaviors as indicators of the child's heart and direction and begin "both to

tear down and to build up" the child.[42]

Though all people need to receive divine wisdom, not everyone will.[43]

Wisdom presents herself as available to three types of individuals: the simple

fool,[44] the ordinary fool, and the wise (those who received understanding and no

---

[38] McKane, 564.

[39] *Betimes*: "from his early days" (Kidner, *Proverbs*, 51, 105).

[40] Waltke, *15-31*, 205. Waltke also emphasizes that Proverbs 22:6 promises the educator or parent that his initial and carefully chosen approach (asking God for wisdom) to educating his child will have a permanent effect on the child for his good.

[41] McKane, 564.

[42] Ibid., 564-65.

[43] Kidner, *Proverbs*, 37-38.

[44] Adams, *CCC Proverbs*, 7; Cohen, 2, 6; Longman, 96.

longer are considered gullible or foolish).[45] Proverbs 1:4-5 states: "To give

prudence to the simple, knowledge and discretion to the youth—Let the wise

hear and increase in learning, and the one who understands obtain guidance."[46]

Kidner states of Proverbs 1:1-5, "Wisdom is the would-be guide of everyman . . .

it is available to the veriest dunce."[47] Similarly, Proverbs 8:1-5 reveals wisdom's

invitation:

> Does not wisdom call? Does not understanding raise her voice? On the heights beside the way, at the crossroads she takes her stand; beside the gates in front of the town, at the entrance of the portals she cries aloud: "To you, O men, I call, and my cry is to the children of man. O simple ones, learn prudence; O fools, learn sense.

With the exception of the scoffer, wisdom presents herself as available to fools

and wise alike.

The Gullible or Young man

In the book of Proverbs two parallel terms are used to describe children:

the *gullible* (*petaim*) and the *young* (*na'ar*; see 22:6).[48] The youth or the gullible are

children from infancy to thirty years of age,[49] and they are all children who are

---

[45] Longman, 98, 197; Kidner, *Proverbs*, 37; Waltke, *1-15*, 111; Cohen, 2. Wiersbe sees Proverbs 1:22 as an invitation from wisdom that includes the scoffer, though no invitation is actually given in this verse (*Be Skillful*, 71). Proverbs 1:22 is more of an introductory definition of each type of fool than it is an invitation to wisdom.

[46] Kidner, *Proverbs*, 37; Longman, 95-97.

[47] Ibid., 76.

[48] Waltke notes, "The parallel to *petaim* [*the gullible*], the *young* (*na'ar*; see 22:6) places the morally brainless *peti* in an age group that extends from infancy (Exod 2:6; 1 Sam 1:22, 24; 4:21) to a seventeen-year-old (Gen. 37:2), to a thirty-year-old (Gen. 41:12; cf. 41:46), and so presumably to any age before being reckoned an *elder* (*zaqen*; see 17:6; 20:29). The distinction pertains as well to the case of inexperience versus experience (cf. 2 Sam 14:21; 18:5; Jer. 1:6)" (Waltke, *1-15*, 178).

[49] Ibid., 178.

immature and without experience or understanding in the world.[50] Waltke

points out, "Though intellectually flawed, the *petaim* 'raw youths,' are the

mildest sorts of fools, for they are malleable, are capable of being shaped and

improved by the educational process (1:4; 8:5; 12:25; 21:11), and still have hope of

joining the company of the wise (cf. 1:22; 9:4)."[51] For it is they, the simple

(*Peᵗā'yim*), who are the object of wisdom's appeal: "Education in wisdom is

offered primarily to the ingenuous youth, who is open to all manner of influence

and in great danger of being led astray."[52]

Though Proverbs has all children in mind,[53] the child in Proverbs whom

the father addresses is a gullible male child most likely moving toward physical

maturity. Waltke states, "In this book the *na'ar* is on the threshold of maturity,

and a decision to join the wise is imperative in order to have the sage's

knowledge."[54] In keeping with Proverbs and the historical context, the father's

address to his older child was not his first time teaching his son divine wisdom.

Waltke points out that in Jewish culture intense teaching began at an early age.

He notes:

---

[50] Cohen, 2; Longman, 96-97; Adams, *CCC Proverbs*, 7. Waltke also notes that this is a youth who lacks sense (*1-15*, 113).

[51] Waltke, *1-15*, 111.

[52] Raymond Edward Brown, Joseph A. Fitzmyer, and Roland Edmund Murphy, *Jerome Biblical Commentary*, vol. 1 (Englewood Cliffs, NJ: Prentice-Hall, 1996), 497.

[53] Murphy states the intended audience of Proverbs and the universal implications. He writes, "It should be emphasized that 'my son' is not to be taken in a gender exclusive sense. This book is for all Israel, and the observations deal with universal human experience, except in very few cases" (Rowland E. Murphy, *Proverbs*, vol. 22 of Word Biblical Commentary [Dallas: Word, 1998], 12).

[54] Ibid., 178.

The father began the stern teaching soon after the child had been weaned, to judge from the example of Samuel (cf. Prov 20:11; 22:6). As soon as Hannah had weaned Samuel, she brought him to the temple at Shiloh, where the high priest Eli immediately began Samuel's tutelage (cf. 1 Sam 1). In the ancient Near East weaning happened after three years of age.[55]

Waltke concludes that Proverbs 4:3 indicates that the child was very young, inexperienced, and completely dependent upon his father and mother when his education began.[56] The wisdom presented in Proverbs was not withheld from the son prior to his moving toward maturity, but was taught to him by Solomon from the earliest of years, just as Solomon had learned from his father.[57] Phillips also sees this important truth:

> Solomon taught his son while he was young to "treasure up" his commands (2:1), knowing that the application might have been a while in coming. Of course we must be wise and age-appropriate. We must not hold a child responsible for what is impossible for their stage of growth (i.e., a ten-month-old probably is not ready to make his bed or empty the trash). At the same time, many parents expect far too little of their children, and thus end up with immature youth. Think of this particularly in terms of obedience. We should start expecting our child to respect and obey us from the earliest reasonable days. I have observed for many years that far too many parents simply do not expect to be obeyed. If a child can obey, then he should be required to obey.[58]

Although parents should not consider most seven-year-olds to be proverbial sluggards, they should recognize that Proverbs has an individual's chosen outlook and destination in view.[59] The child may not be a sluggard or a scorner, but their slothful attitude and behaviors reveal the direction of their

---

[55] Ibid., 277-78.

[56] Ibid., 278; Tedd Tripp compares the ordinary fool's desires and fears to the normal vocabulary of a three-year-old. He goes on to point out that all children are born with a heart of folly (106).

[57] Kidner, *Proverbs*, 51, 105.

[58] Phillips, 283.

[59] "It must always be remembered that the book has in mind a man's chosen outlook" Kidner, *Proverbs*, 40); see also Longman, 300.

138

heart. Often society thinks of child-like behavior as reflecting the child's immaturity, but Proverbs sees these behaviors as indicating the child's direction if not turned from his natural way. Tripp writes:

> The other pitfall is an inability to work from behavior to the appropriate character issues. This results in seeing only isolated bits of behavior. The result again is failure to address long-term character goals. . . . You must be a person of long-term vision. You must see your children's need for shepherding, not simply in terms of the here and now, but in terms of long-range vision.[60]

In other words, the child's behavior reveals his heart's direction and the person he is becoming.

Without a change of heart, the child's natural course is to follow his foolish/immature heart. Foolishness is in fact bound in the heart of every child (Prov 22:15)[61]: they are undisciplined, inexperienced, and without knowledge, so they act accordingly. Foolishness in verse 15, "refers to delinquency which is here said to be bound up in a child, i.e., a natural state in the early period of life."[62] Much of what is considered to be normal child-like immaturity in relation to ADHD behaviors is actually behavior that reflects a foolish heart, which Proverbs also addresses. Longman writes:

> One important purpose of the book is to give prudence to the simpleminded. Parallel to this is the intention to give knowledge and discretion to the "young" (na'ar). The na'ar usually is chronologically young, typically an adolescent and unmarried, though in any case, another nuance of the word might also come into play in the present context, and that is 'immature.' The na'ar is immature and needs the knowledge and discretion that will be provided by the book of Proverbs.[63]

---

[60] Tripp, 181-82.

[61] Ibid., 51; Waltke, *1-15*, 111; Waltke, *15-31*, 215-16; McKane, 564-65.

[62] Cohen, 148.

[63] Longman, 97.

Parents cannot assume that the simple child will grow out of immature habits (foolishness), but instead, they must practice biblical parental discipline and impart prudence to their children.[64] Kidner discusses both aspects of biblical parental discipline in his study of the word *wisdom* and states, "The two terms [*instruction* and *correction*] together can be summed up as *discipline*" [65] The common juxtaposition of the simple fool and the prudent is important in Proverbs (e.g., Proverbs 14:18 where each is known by his heart's condition). The simple fool is known by his stupidity, and the prudent child is honored for his observable knowledge.[66] If left to himself, the simple fool will "metaphorically" inherit foolishness.[67] In other words, he will end up being as immature as when he first began. Trusting in his own way has left him with all that his heart possesses—his own foolishness. The one who receives moral truths, however, will inherit honor and dignity.[68]

Solomon's son is not presented in Proverbs as a sluggard, an ordinary fool, or a scorner, yet his father still warned him not to choose those outlooks and ways of life. The same is true with young children. Children as young as three or

---

[64] "'Prudence' describes one's ability to use reason, in context under the fear of God, to navigate the problems of life. Prudence carefully considers a situation before rushing in. It implies cool headedness" (Longman, 97). Prudence addresses the child's impulsivity, lack of self-control, and immaturity directly. Divine wisdom gives the student *knowledge* and *prudence,* which allow him to "walk the path of life in a constructive way and to avoid the lures of the evil path (Prov 2:11)" (ibid.).

[65] *Proverbs*, 36.

[66] The *crown* is a typical metaphor in Proverbs for honor. This passage implies that behaviors that are produced from the heart are in mind, since others can discern what is in the child's heart (Longman, 302-3; Steveson, 191).

[67] Kidner, *Proverbs*, 109.

[68] Waltke, *1-15*, 596-97.

140

four years of age can be taught and can understand important wisdom that is relevant to their immediate lives as well as warning them of the destination of their natural way. Immaturity is expected from the foolish heart, but the application of wisdom will drive it far from him.

Scripture gives parents the wisdom necessary to approach all types of children. Young children who are diagnosed with ADHD (whether saved or unsaved) are most likely immature[69] and simple, but though lacking understanding, they have a teachable spirit[70] which allows them to hear wisdom (Prov 1:8; 14:18)[71] and to receive correction (Prov 20:30; 22:15; 23:14).[72] Scripture provides several ways that parents can impart divine wisdom to their children, yet two methods, the rod and reproof, are named specifically in Proverbs for addressing child-like foolishness. Jay Adams notes that both the rod and reproof are necessary to impart wisdom. He states, "Reproof alone is insufficient, as is the rod alone. Both must be used if discipline is to succeed. Wisdom comes from the balanced use of the two in tandem."[73] Thus the rod and reproof are not only vital to a simple child's moral education, but also functional in his life

---

[69] Secularists also recognize this characteristic. See Paul Wender, *ADHD: Attention-Deficit Hyperactivity Disorder in Children, Adolescents, and Adults* (New York: Oxford University Press, 2000), 28.

[70] Kidner, *Proverbs*, 39.

[71] Longman, 302-3; Waltke, *1-15*, 596-97.

[72] Kidner, *Proverbs*, 141; Cohen, 137, 148, 154; Kidner, *Proverbs*, 152; Waltke, *15-31*, 251-53

[73] Adams, *CCC Proverbs*, 217.

(Prov 10:13; 22:15; 29:15).[74] Waltke writes concerning Proverbs 19:18 and the

father's need to place hope in wise discipline,

> The imprecise antithetical parallels imply that the father's hope in discipline is to impart to his clinical offspring eternal life, the opposite of death, and that a failure to discipline the son is tantamount to participating in killing him (cf. 11:7, 23; 13:24; 20:30; 22:6, 15; 23:13, 14; 29:15)....The proverb assumes both that folly is bound up in the heart of the child, and that the rod of discipline will drive it far from him (22:15).[75]

Parents can only encourage children to choose divine wisdom; they

cannot force it upon them. No amount of pressure, pain, or lectures will be

enough to change the child's heart (Prov 27:22).[76] Ultimately, the child is

responsible to choose the path that he will take in life—whether wisdom or folly.

The Wise

As with a child or young adult without wisdom, the one who has already

received divine wisdom (a believer) needs to continue to acquire it.[77] Longman

states:

> Wisdom is not gained by a onetime decision, but a decision followed by a lifetime of discipline. It is a rigorous endeavor, involving study a well as self-control, especially in light of the apparent rewards from going on the easier path of the wicked.[78]

---

[74] Adams points out the error in many secular studies that only consider the rod apart from biblical reproof: "When you read studies in which it is said that corporal punishment fails, ask whether the studies had anything to do with the joint activities always advised in the Word of God. You can be sure that they do not" (*CCC Proverbs*, 217); Waltke writes, "Fools must be corrected both by caning and by rebuke (see also 26:3-5). They cannot save themselves because they return to their folly as dogs to vomit (26:11)" (Waltke, *1-15*, 461-62). For more on the rod of discipline, see Lou Priolo, *Teach Them Diligently: How to Use the Scriptures in Child Training* (Woodruff, S.C.: Timeless Texts, 2000) 95-100.

[75] Waltke, *15-31*, 112.

[76] Kidner, *Proverbs*, 51; Wiersbe, *Be Skillful*, 79.

[77] Adams, *CCC Proverbs*, 7; Kidner, *Proverbs*, 38; Cohen, 2.

[78] Longman, 152.

The wise must continue to receive wisdom. This reality is specifically applicable when parents have a young child who has been diagnosed with ADHD and has also made a profession of faith. Many times it can be unclear if his salvation decision was genuine or not, since his lifestyle is characterized by frequent participation in foolish behavior. In other words, he is not merely engaging in foolish behavior every so often as young children do, but is known by his foolish behaviors. As was noted previously from Ephesians 5:17, believers can behave foolishly if they lack understanding or choose to live according to their natural way. Parents should expect that younger children who profess to know God will still behave foolishly at times, which the rod and reproof can remedy. A child who is in the company of the wise will respond to correction and reproof differently than a simpleton, an ordinary fool, or a scorner. Whether the child is a simpleton or in the company of the wise, parents need to earnestly teach and admonish since both types of children need and can receive God's wisdom.

The Ordinary Fool

Unlike the simple who is gullible, the ordinary or stupid fool is consumed with his own opinion (Prov 15:28)[79] and, to his own peril, perceives that he does not need advice (Prov 14:12).[80] In essence, he views his wisdom as more important than God's wisdom, and he acts in accordance. Whereas the scorner hates reproof (Proverbs 9:7-8),[81] the ordinary fool does not always hate those

---

[79] His high opinion of his own thoughts cause him to be impulsive and blurt out his own opinion that is contrary to wisdom (Longman, 322); see also Kidner, *Proverbs*, 40.

[80] Waltke, *1-15*, 533; Cohen writes that the fool is "defined as one who is 'insensible to moral truth and acts without regard to it'" (6); see also Kidner, *Proverbs*, 108.

[81] Ibid., 114; Cohen, 53.

who confront him. Instead, he ignores, rejects, or does not benefit from the rod, rebuke, and correction (Prov 17:10).[82] Proverbs 26:4-5 indicates that parents must discern how to best approach a fool. For the fool's own sake, parents should not always engage him (Prov 26:4). Yet lest he become prouder and potentially harden his heart beyond hope, parents should sometimes give him an answer (Prov 26:5).[83]

The Scoffer

In contrast to the natural fool (simple) and the ordinary fool, the scoffer has arrogantly (Prov 21:24)[84] made up his mind that he wants nothing to do with God, his wisdom, or those of like-mind (Prov 13:1).[85] In fact, he not only despises God's wisdom (Prov 23:9)[86] and those who attempt to reprove and correct him (Prov 9:7-8),[87] he is bent on leading others away from divine truth (Prov 21:24).[88]

---

[82] Waltke, *1-15*, 111; Cohen, 113. In the New Testament, Peter refers to Proverbs 26:11 in stating that it is better for the fool (in this context the *fool* refers to the apostate who once appeared to be a believer; D. Edmond Hiebert, *Second Peter and Jude* [Greenville, S.C.: Bob Jones University Press, 1989], 133.) if he had not even heard of the way of righteousness (remained simple), than to have seemingly embraced it and then to have turned his back on the sacred command (2 Pet 2:20-22). This warning does not imply that the simple are not culpable for their lack of understanding, only that there are worse eternal consequences for the one who deliberately rejects or ignores God's wisdom.

[83] Waltke, *15-31*, 349-50; Kidner, *Proverbs*, 162.

[84] Cohen, 142; Waltke, *1-15*, 114; Wiersbe, *Be Skillful*, 73-74.

[85] Kidner, *Proverbs*, 42; Waltke, *1-15*, 551; Cohen, 80.

[86] Waltke, *1-15*, 181; Cohen, 153.

[87] Wiersbe, *Be Skillful*, 73; Cohen, 53-54.

[88] Kidner writes concerning this type of fool that he is a "deliberate trouble-maker (Prov 21:24; 22:10; 29:9). He impresses the impressionable, as long as he is allowed in his way (19:25; 21:11)" (*Proverbs*, 42). Waltke also points out that the simple or gullible is being targeted educationally by both the wicked and the wise (*1-15*, 111).

Though he may hate those who wisely confront him, there is potential benefit to the simple to see the hardened fool confronted and corrected (Prov 19:25).[89] Though it may be rare for a child as young as twelve years old to become an ordinary fool or a scorner, it is possible that a child this young could hate God and his wisdom.[90] Scripture does not place age limitations on who can be a simpleton, an ordinary fool, or a scoffer but always bases one's position upon his or her treatment and understanding of divine wisdom. Since ODD behaviors[91] can in fact, reveal a hardened heart in older children, parents and counselors should not exclude the consideration that a middle-school-aged child or older may already hate divine wisdom and established authority.

The Heart Rather Than Behaviors

The heart of man remains the core issue, and behaviors are merely its product. As is discussed in the main body of this book, the human tendency is to judge children and others by their observable and repeated behaviors and then to label them (e.g., one who paints repeatedly is called a painter, and one who smokes is labeled as a smoker). The behaviors of the fool, however, do not make him a fool but reveal what he is. Waltke states this reality concisely: "A wise heart produces righteous behavior, and a foolish heart produces wicked behavior."[92] Additionally, though differences exist among them, all three types

---

[89] Kidner, *Proverbs*, 39; Wiersbe, *Be Skillful*, 73.

[90] Tripp discusses that if foolishness is permitted to grow in the heart of a child, by the time he is a teenager, he may be rebellious and "not allow anyone to rule him"(106).

[91] For Barkley's description of ODD behaviors, see Russell A. Barkley, *Taking Charge of ADHD: A Complete Authoritative Guide for Parents*, rev. ed. (New York: Guilford, 2000), 169.

[92] Waltke, *1-15*, 93.

of fools have similarly foolish mindsets and behaviors. For example, Kidner points out that to the simple fool "folly is fun (Prov 15:21)" and the ordinary fool, in the same way, "likes his folly (Prov 20:4)."[93] As the heart becomes more hardened, a pattern of foolish behavior typically becomes more distinguished as observable rebellion.[94]

Teenagers who are from believing families and are diagnosed with ADHD because of their disobedience and complacency most likely fall into the second category of fools. This generality assumes that parents are walking with God and have diligently and wisely corrected and instructed, yet these children have chosen to ignore divine wisdom and, instead, live foolishly.

Although Proverbs' principle discussion is on moral education (divine and practical wisdom), the book's consideration also includes temporal instructions from authorities (such as a parent commanding the son to stay seated).[95] The child must obey his parents because all authority in his life is established by God and represents God's authority (Rom 13:1-5).[96] If a child who

---

[93] Kidner, *Proverbs*, 39-40.

[94] Generally speaking, a child is known by his behaviors, but the very essence of a hypocrite is one who acts differently than the true nature of his heart (s.v. "hypocrite"; available from http://www.merriam-webster.com/dictionary/ hypocrite; Internet: accessed 14 April 2014). Although behaviors can reveal the heart, parents should be careful to not make the mistake of assuming a young child, whose behavior is seemingly out of control to be scornful or rebellious. Likewise, an older child who is calm and not hyper, loud, or destructive may still be a scorner at heart. Therefore, you should discern by your child's treatment of God's wisdom rather than by merely their behaviors as to their position before God.

[95] Waltke, *1-15*, 352.

[96] The context of Romans 13 is speaking of political authorities, yet all authority, including parental authority, is established by God. Hodge writes, "**Governing authorities** means those in authority without reference to their status or character. We are to be subject not only to the *supreme* authorities, but to all who have authority over us. The abstract word

is able to understand, rejects his parents' temporal commands, he is in essence rejecting God's wisdom, since God expects him to honor and obey his parents (Eph 6:1-3). Tedd Tripp sees the connection between the child's obedience to his parents and his obedience to God: "It is a question of authority. Will the child live under the authority of God and therefore the authority of his parents, or under his own authority — driven by his wants and passions?"[97]

Because of this God-given authority, parents and teachers who instruct a child diagnosed with ADHD to remain in his seat should expect him to obey, if he is of an age that he is able to understand. Obedience to authority in all areas of life, then, must be connected ultimately by the parents to the child's acceptance of God's wisdom by faith. Believing parents should want their children to obey them, but for the right reason. The Jewish commentator Cohen notes the teacher's emphasis on appealing to the heart rather than merely focusing on behavior. He writes:

> This saying [Proverbs 17:10] well illustrates how the efforts of the Wisdom writers were concentrated on the appeal to the inner man, i.e., on the foundation of character, the most essential part of education. Here the writer states the widely recognized fact of the sensitiveness, in the best sense, of refined and exalted character in contrast to the thick-skinned unimpressionableness of a 'fool.'[98]

---

authorities is used for those who are invested with power (Luke 12:11; Ephesians 1:21; 3:10; etc.). The word **governing** is applied to anyone who is greater than us in dignity and authority. In 1 Peter 2:13 it is applied to the king as supreme — that is, superior to all other governing authorities" (Charles Hodge, *Romans*, Crossway Classic Commentaries [Wheaton: Crossway, 1993], Ro 13:1). See also James D. G. Dunn, *Romans 9–16*, vol. 38B of Word Biblical Commentary (Dallas: Word, 1998), 771; F. F. Bruce, *Romans: An Introduction and Commentary*, vol. 6 of Tyndale New Testament Commentaries (Downers Grove: InterVarsity, 1985), 235–37.

[97] Earlier in the same section, Tripp writes that a fool is one who lives according to his wants and desires and that this reality qualifies all unsaved children as fools (106).

[98] Cohen, 113.

The time will come in every child's life that obedience to parents will no longer be necessary: when he is mature and leaves his father and mother. The true authority, however, under which he obeyed them remains over his life. The heart of the child must be educated, rather than temporarily controlled. If parents do not teach their children to please God as the right motivation to obey their God ordained authorities, then they fail in one aspect to teach their children divine wisdom. If parents have taught their teen the right motivation for obedience, then for the child to disobey repeatedly is evidence of the child's foolish rejection of God's wisdom as well.

Again, it is important to stress that it is the natural tendency of a young child who is still teachable to forget instruction and repeat folly. He most likely is an immature simpleton who needs discipline rather than an ordinary fool who is apathetic. As he gets older and continues to ignore godly parental instruction, however, he begins to distinguish himself as an ordinary fool and not just one who is gullible.

Conclusion

When Scripture refers to someone as a fool, it does not imply that he lacks intelligence, but that he lacks divine wisdom. Though it is best to not call a child a *fool*, the biblical concepts are nonetheless key to right anthropology and to both understanding and helping the child whom secularists have diagnosed as having ADHD.

APPENDIX B: "OFTEN TALKS EXCESSIVELY" WORKSHEET

INSTRUCTIONS: Name: _____

☐ *Please read the following passages of Scripture, copy them onto another paper, and then answer the questions below:*

Proverbs 10:19-20; 13:3

Proverbs 14:3; 15:2

Proverbs 16:23; 17:27-28

Proverbs 18:7; 29:20 - *Memorize*

James 1:26

QUESTIONS:

1. Where do the words of one's mouth come from?

2. What do one's words reveal about the heart?

3. What are the characteristics of a wicked man's mouth?

4. What does Scripture say about someone who cannot control his mouth?

5. What does Scripture say about people who say they love God, yet they do not control their tongue?

6. Are one's words important to God? If they are, why or why not?

7. Why do you think it displeases God when you say everything that you think?

APPENDIX C: "IMPULSIVITY" WORKSHEET

INSTRUCTIONS: Name: _____

☐ *This week: Memorize Philippians 2:2-5*

☐ *Please read the following passages of Scripture together with your child, and then answer the questions below:*

STUDY VERSES:

1. "Often blurts out answers before questions have been finished" Prov. 18:13; 29:20

2. "Often has trouble waiting one's turn" Prov. 16:32; 1 Cor. 13:4a; Gal. 5:16-24

3. "Often interrupts or intrudes on others" Prov. 17:27; Phil. 2:2-5; James 1:26

QUESTIONS:

1. How does God view your lack of control and behavior?

2. What are some common words that you noticed in the above verses that describe the heart of these behaviors?

3. According to the above verses, how can you overcome your naturally selfish heart?

4. According to the above verses, when you interrupt others or are not willing to wait your turn, whose needs are you looking out for?

5. Write at least two things that need to change in your life.

APPENDIX D: THE HEART OF DISOBEDIENCE WORKSHEET

INSTRUCTIONS: Name: _____

☐ *This week: Memorize Ephesians 6:1-3*

☐ *Please read the following verses then answer the questions below on a separate sheet of paper.*

STUDY VERSES:

"Often <u>does not follow through with instruction</u> and fails to finish things."

Proverbs 4:1-2; 6:6-11; 10:4-5, 26; 15:19; 20:4

"Often fidgets with hands and feet or squirms in seat <u>when expected</u> to sit still."

Colossians 3:20

"Often gets up from seat <u>when expected</u> to be seated." Ephesians 6:1-3

"Often excessively runs about or climbs <u>when and where it is not appropriate</u>."

Proverbs 25:28; Colossians 3:20

QUESTIONS:

1. How does God view a child's not listening to his parents' instructions (theology)?

3. When you disobey your parents, what do you reveal about your heart

(anthropology)?

4. What steps can you take in your life to overcome your disobedient heart (application)?

5. According to the above verses, does it please God to obey your authority's commands

but with a wrong attitude or motive?

APPENDIX E: THE HEART OF ANGER WORKSHEET

INSTRUCTIONS: Name: _____

☐ *This week: Memorize James 1:19-20 and Proverbs 14:29*

☐ *Please read the following verses then answer the questions below on separate paper.*

STUDY VERSES:

1. Proverbs 15:1; 29:22

2. Proverbs 14:29; 19:11

3. Galatians 5:16-24

4. Ephesians 4:26, 31-32

5. James 1:19-20; 4:1-6

QUESTIONS:

1. How does God view man's anger and violence (theology)?

2. When you are angry in your heart or you act out in anger or violence,   what do you reveal about your heart (anthropology)?

3. What steps can you take in your life to overcome your naturally angry heart (application)?

4. According to the above verses, why do you get angry (motives)?

151

SELECTED BIBLIOGRAPHY

Adams, Jay. *Back to the Blackboard: Design for a Biblical Christian School.* Phillipsburg, N.J.: Presbyterian and Reformed, 1982.

————. *The Big Umbrella and Other Essays and Addresses on Christian Counseling.* Grand Rapids: Baker, 1972.

————. *The Christian Counselor's Commentary: Proverbs.* Woodruff, S.C.: Timeless Texts, 1997.

————. *Christian Counselor's Commentary: Romans, Philippians, 1 Thessalonians, and 2 Thessalonians.* Woodruff, S.C.: Timeless Texts, 1995.

————. *The Christian Counselor's Manual.* Phillipsburg, N.J.: Presbyterian and Reformed, 1973.

————. *Competent to Counsel: Introduction to Nouthetic Counseling.* Grand Rapids: Zondervan, 1970.

————. *More than Redemption: A Theology of Christian Counseling.* Grand Rapids: Baker, 1979.

————. "Spiritual Counseling Is Spiritual," *Bibliotheca Sacra* 131 (1974).

Alexander, T. Desmond, Brian S. Rosner, D. A. Carson, and Graeme Goldsworthy, eds. *New Dictionary of Biblical Theology.* Westmont, Ill.: InterVarsity, 2000.

American Academy of Pediatrics. "Clinical Practice Guideline for the Diagnosis, Evaluation, and Treatment of Attention-Deficit/Hyperactivity Disorder in Children and Adolescents." Available from http://pediatrics.aappublications.org/content/early/2011/10/14/peds.2011-2654. Internet; accessed 23 April 2012.

American Psychological Association. *Diagnostic Criteria from the DSM-IV-TR.* Washington, D.C.: American Psychiatric Association, 2000.

Arnsten, Amy F. T., Mary V. Solanto, and F. Xavier Castellanos, eds. *Stimulant Drugs and ADHD: Basic and Clinical Neuroscience.* New York: Oxford University Press, 2001.

Atkison, David. *The Message of Proverbs.* Downers Grove: InterVarsity, 1996.

Barkley, Russell. "ADD, ODD, Emotional Impulsiveness, and Relationships." Available from http://www.youtube.com/watch?v=rcwp9T3zNcM&feature=related. Internet; accessed 4 March 2012.

————. *ADHD and the Nature of Self-Control.* New York: Guilford, 2005.

————. "ADHD Intention Deficit Disorder." Available from http://www.youtube.com/watch?v=wF1YRE8ff1g. Internet; accessed 28 February 2012.

————. "ADHD — To Medicate or Not?" Available from http://www.youtube.com/watch?v=V724jfgabKE&feature=related. Internet; accessed 27 February 2012.

————. *Defiant Children: A Clinician's Manual for Assessment and Parent Training.* 2nd ed. New York: Guilford, 1997.

————. *Taking Charge of ADHD: A Complete, Authoritative Guide for Parents.* Rev. ed. New York: Guilford, 2000.

Barkley, Russell A., Kevin R. Murphy, and Mariellen Fischer. *ADHD in Adults: What the Science Says.* New York: Guilford, 2008.

BBC News. "Bad Behaviour 'Linked to Smoking.'" Available from http://news.bbc.co.uk/2/hi/health/4727197.stm. Internet; accessed 10 August 2010.

Beale, G. K., and D. A. Carson, eds. *Commentary on the New Testament Use of the Old Testament.* Grand Rapids: Baker, 2007.

Benedek, Elissa P. Review of *ADHD in Adults: What the Science Says,* by Russell A. Barkley, Kevin Murphy, and Mariellen Fischer. *Bulletin of the Menninger Clinic* 73, no. 1 (Winter 2009).

Benner, David, ed. *Baker Encyclopedia of Psychology.* Grand Rapids: Baker, 1985.

Benner, David and Peter Hill, eds. *Baker Encyclopedia of Psychology and Counseling.* 2nd ed. Grand Rapids: Baker, 1999.

Boice, James Montgomery. *Psalms 107-150.* Vol. 3 of *Psalms.* Expositional Commentary. Grand Rapids: Baker, 1998.

154

Boyd, Carrie Anne. "The Role of Music in Counseling and Discipleship." Master's thesis, Master's College, 2002.

Boyles, Salynn. "Immaturity Mistaken for ADHD? Youngest Kids in Classroom More Likely to Be Diagnosed." *WebMD Health News.* Available from http://children.webmd.com/news/20120305/is-immaturity-being-mistaken-adhd?ecd=wnl_prg_031112. Internet; accessed 9 March 2012.

Breggin, Peter. "Medication Madness: The Role of Psychiatric Drugs in Cases of Violence, Suicide and Murder." Available from http://www.breggin.com/index.php?option=com_content&task=view&id=55&Itemid=79. Internet; accessed 12 July 2012.

————. *Toxic Psychiatry.* New York: St. Martin's Press, 1991.

Breggin, Peter, and Ginger Breggin. "The Hazards of Treating 'Attention-Deficit/Hyperactivity Disorder' with Methylphenidate (Ritalin)." *Journal of College Students Psychotherapy* 10, no. 2 (1995): 55-72.

Brice, P. J. "The Experience of Learning for Youth Diagnosed with Attention Deficit Hyperactivity Disorder." PhD diss., Union Institute and University, 1998.

Bruce, F. F. *Romans: An Introduction and Commentary.* Vol. 6 of Tyndale New Testament Commentaries. Downers Grove: InterVarsity, 1985.

Bubble, Mark, Barry Duncan, and Scott Miller. *The Heart and Soul of Change: What Works in Therapy.* Washington, D.C.: American Psychological Association, 1999.

Calvin, John. *Acts.* Vol. 10 of Crossway Classic Commentaries. Edited by Alister McGrath and J. I. Packer. Wheaton: Crossway, 1995.

————. *Commentaries on the Book of the Prophet Jeremiah and the Lamentations.* vol. 2. Translated and edited by John Owen. Edinburgh: Calvin Translation Society, 1851.

————. *Commentaries on the Catholic Epistles.* Translated and edited by John Owen. Edinburgh: Calvin Translation Society, 1855.

————. *Commentaries on the Epistle of Paul the Apostle to the Romans.* Translated and edited by John Owen. Edinburgh: Calvin Translation Society, 1849.

————. *Commentary on the Book of Psalms*, vol. 2. Translated by James Anderson. Edinburgh: Calvin Translation Society, 1846.

————. *Genesis.* Vol. 25 of Crossway Classic Commentaries. Edited by Alister McGrath and J.I. Packer, Wheaton: Crossway, 2001.

————. *Isaiah.* Vol. 24 of Crossway Classic Commentaries. Edited by Alister McGrath and J. I. Packer. Wheaton: Crossway, 2000.

155

————. *John*. Vol. 5 of Crossway Classic Commentaries. Edited by Alister McGrath and J. I. Packer. Wheaton: Crossway, 1994.

Carey, William B. "What to Do about the ADHD Epidemic." *American Academy of Pediatrics: Developmental and Behavioral Pediatrics Newsletter* (Autumn 2003): 6-7. Available from http://www.ahrp.org/children/CareyADHD0603.php. Internet; accessed 3 May 2012.

Cherry, Kendra. "Social Learning Theory: An Overview of Bandura's Social Learning Theory." Available from http://psychology.about.com/od/developmentalpsychology/a/sociallearning.htm. Internet; accessed 2 September 2012.

Chriss, James J. *Social Control: An Introduction*. Cambridge: Polity, 2007.

Christensen, Duane L. *Deuteronomy 1–21:9*. Vol. 6A of Word Biblical Commentary. Dallas: Word, 2001.

Clines, David J. A. *Job 21–37*. Vol. 18a of Word Biblical Commentary. Nashville: Thomas Nelson, 2006.

Cohen, Abraham. *Proverbs*. London: Soncino Press, 1973.

Collingwood, Jane. "The Genetics of ADHD." Available from http://psychcentral.com/lib/2010/the-genetics-of-adhd. Internet; accessed 16 September 2010.

Cousins, Leigh Pretnar. "Might Schools Be Teaching ADHD?" Available from http://psychcentral.com/lib/2010/might-schools-be-teaching-adhd/. Internet; accessed 16 September 2010.

Curwin, Richard L., Allen N. Mendler, and Brian D. Mendler. *Discipline with Dignity: New Challenges, New Solutions*. 3rd ed. Alexandria, Va.: Association for Supervision and Curriculum Development, 2008.

Denoon, Daniel. "Kids' Poor Bedtime Habits May Bring ADHD Misdiagnosis." Available from http://www.webmd.com/add-adhd/news/20110919/kids-poor-bedtime-habits-may-bring-adhd-misdiagnosis. Internet; accessed 23 September 2011.

Easton, M. G. *Easton's Bible Dictionary*. New York: Harper and Brothers, 1893.

Ellingworth, Paul. *The Epistle to the Hebrews*. New International Greek Testament Commentary. Grand Rapids: Eerdmans, 1993.

Ellison, Katherine. "Brain Scans Link ADHD to Biological Flaw Tied to Motivation." Available from http://www.washingtonpost.com/wpdyn/content/article/2009/09/21/AR2009092103100.html. Internet; accessed 22 September 2010.

Elwell, Walter A., ed. *Baker Encyclopedia of the Bible*. 4 vols. Grand Rapids: Baker, 1997.

English Standard Version. Wheaton: Good News, 2001.

Erickson, Millard J. *Christian Theology*. 2nd ed. Grand Rapids: Baker, 1999.

Fletcher-Janzen, Elaine, and Cecil Reynolds, eds. *Disorders Diagnostic Desk Reference*. Hoboken, N.J.: John Wiley and Sons, Inc., 2003.

Flora, Stephen. *Taking America off Drugs: Why Behavioral Therapy is More Effective for Treating ADHD, OCD, Depression, and Other Psychological Problems*. Alba, N.Y.: State University of New York Press, 2007.

Foulkes, Francis. *Ephesians*. Rev. ed. Vol. 10 of Tyndale New Testament Commentaries. Grand Rapids: Eerdmans, 1989.

Fronmüller, G.F.C. and J. Isidor Mombert. *The First Epistle General of Peter*. Vol. 9 of *Lange's Commentary on the Holy Scriptures*. Translated and edited by Philip Schaff. 1871; reprint, Grand Rapids: Zondervan, n.d.

————. *The Second Epistle General of Peter*. Vol. 9 of *Lange's Commentary on the Holy Scriptures*. Translated and edited by Philip Schaff. 1871; reprint, Grand Rapids: Zondervan, n.d.

Generation RX. DVD. Directed by Kevin Miller. Vancouver: Common Radius Films, 2008.

Goldstein, Sam, and Barbara Ingersoll. *Attention Deficit Disorder and Learning Disabilities: Realities, Myths and Controversial Treatments*. New York: Double Day Publications, 1993.

Gray, Peter. "The 'ADHD Personality': Its Cognitive, Biological, and Evolutionary Foundations." Available from http://www.psychologytoday.com/blog/freedom-learn/201008/the-adhd-personality-its-cognitive-biological-and-evolutionary-foundations. Internet; accessed 15 September 2010.

Grudem, Wayne A. *1 Peter: An Introduction and Commentary*. Vol. 17 of Tyndale New Testament Commentaries. Downers Grove: InterVarsity, 1988.

Guelich, Robert A. *Mark 1–8:26*. Vol. 34A of Word Biblical Commentary. Dallas: Word, 1998.

Guthrie, Donald. *Hebrews: An Introduction and Commentary*. Vol. 15 of Tyndale New Testament Commentaries. Downers Grove: InterVarsity, 1983.

Guthrie, Donald. *Pastoral Epistles: An Introduction and Commentary*. Vol. 14 of Tyndale New Testament Commentaries. Downers Grove: InterVarsity, 1990.

Haber, Julian. *ADHD: The Great Misdiagnosis*. New York: Taylor Trade, 2003.

157

Hallowell, Edward M. "Dr. Hallowell's Response to NY Times Piece 'Ritalin Gone Wrong.'" Available from http://www.drhallowell.com/blog/dr-hallowells-response-to-ny-times-piece-ritalin-gone-wrong/. Internet; accessed 10 August 2012.

Hallowell, Edward M., and John J. Ratey. *Delivered from Distraction: Getting the Most out of Life with Attention Deficit Disorder.* New York: Ballantine Books, 2005.

————. *Driven to Distraction: Recognizing and Coping with Attention Deficit Disorder from Childhood through Adulthood.* New York: Pantheon Books, 1994.

Hartwell-Walker, Marie. "It May Not Be ADHD." Available from http://psychcentral.com/lib/2010/it-may-not-be-adhd. Internet; accessed 16 September 2010.

Hendriksen, William, and Simon J. Kistemaker. *Exposition of the Gospel According to Luke.* Vol. 11 of New Testament Commentary. Grand Rapids: Baker, 2012.

————.*Exposition of the Gospel According to Matthew.* Vol. 9 of New Testament Commentary. Grand Rapids: Baker, 1973.

————. *Exposition of Philippians.* Vol. 5 of New Testament Commentary. Grand Rapids: Baker Book House, 2012.

Hodge, Charles. *1 Corinthians.* Vol. 11 of Crossway Classic Commentaries. Edited by Alister McGrath and J. I. Packer. Wheaton: Crossway, 1995.

————. *2 Corinthians.* Vol. 12 of Crossway Classic Commentaries. Edited by Alister McGrath and J. I. Packer. Wheaton: Crossway, 1995.

————. *Ephesians.* Vol. 7 of Crossway Classic Commentaries. Edited by Alister McGrath and J.I. Packer. Wheaton: Crossway, 1994.

————. *Romans.* Crossway Classic Commentaries. Edited by Alister McGrath and J.I. Packer. Wheaton: Crossway, 1993.

Hubbard, D. A. *Proverbs.* Dallas: Word, 1989.

Hughes, P. E. "The Priesthood of Believers." *Evangelical Dictionary of Theology.* Edited by Walter A. Elwell. Grand Rapids: Baker, 1996.

HealthBulletin News Archive. "Risky Ritalin Abuse during College Exam Week." Available from http://ihealthbulletin.com/archive/2007/05/14/risky-ritalin-abuse-during-college-exam-week/. Internet; accessed 17 September 2010.

158

Insel, Thomas. "Brain Scans: Not Quite Ready for Prime Time." Available from http://www.nimh.nih.gov/about/director/index-adhd.shtml. Internet; accessed 4 May 2013.

————. "Transforming Diagnosis." Available from http://www.nimh.nih.gov/about/director/2013/transforming-diagnosis.shtml. Internet; accessed 4 May 2013.

Jamieson, Robert, A. R. Fausset, and David Brown. *Commentary Critical and Explanatory on the Whole Bible.* Peabody: Hendrickson Publishers Marketing, 1996.

Jenni, Ernst, and Claus Westermann. *Theological Lexicon of the Old Testament.* Peabody, Mass.: Hendrickson, 1997.

Johnston C., and E. J. Mash. "Families of Children with Attention Deficit/Hyperactivity Disorder: Review and Recommendations for Future Research." *Clinical Child Family Psychology* 4:3 (2001): 183-207.

Kidner, Derek. *Proverbs: An Introduction and Commentary.* Tyndale Old Testament Commentaries. Edited by Donald J. Wiseman. Downers Grove: InterVarsity, 1975.

Kidner, Derek. *Psalms 73–150: An Introduction and Commentary.* Vol. 16 of Tyndale Old Testament Commentaries. Edited by Donald J. Wiseman. Downers Grove: InterVarsity, 1975.

Kohn, Alfie. *Beyond Discipline: From Compliance to Community.* 10th anniversary ed. Alexandria, Va.: Association for Supervision and Curriculum Development, 2006.

Kruse, Colin G. *2 Corinthians: An Introduction and Commentary.* Vol. 8 of Tyndale New Testament Commentaries. Downers Grove: InterVarsity Press, 1987.

————. *John: An Introduction and Commentary.* Vol. 4 of Tyndale New Testament Commentaries. Downers Grove: InterVarsity, 2003.

Lane, Christopher. "The NIMH Withdraws Support for the *DSM-5*." Available from http://www.psychologytoday.com/blog/side-effects/201305/the-nimh-withdraws-support-dsm-5. Internet; accessed 4 May 2013.

Lane, William L. *Hebrews 9–13.* Vol. 47B of Word Biblical Commentary. Dallas: Word, 1998.

Lange, John Peter. *Genesis.* Translated and edited by Tayler Lewis and A. Gosman. Old Testament Vol. 1 of *Lange's Commentary on the Holy Scriptures.* Edited by Philip Schaff. 1857; reprint, Grand Rapids: Zondervan, n.d.

————. *The Gospel According to Matthew.* Translated and edited by Philip Schaff. New Testament Vol. 1 of *Lange's A Commentary on the Holy Scriptures.* Edited by Philip Schaff. 1889; reprint, Grand Rapids: Zondervan, n.d.

159

Langston, Evelyn. *Lord, Help Me Love This Hyperactive Child*. Nashville: Broadman, 1992.

Larimore, Walt. "Facts about ADHD." Available from http://www.focusonthe family.com/parenting/parenting_challenges/ adhd/facts_about_adhd .aspx. Internet; accessed 20 February 2012.

Liefeld, Walter. *Ephesians*. IVP New Testament Commentary Series. Edited by Grant R. Osborne. Downers Grove: InterVarsity, 1997.

Lightfoot, Joseph Barber. *Colossians and Philemon*. Vol. 13 of Crossway Classic Commentaries. Edited by Alister McGrath and J. I. Packer. Wheaton: Crossway Books, 1997.

————. *Philippians*. Vol. 8 of Crossway Classic Commentaries. Edited by Alister McGrath and J. I. Packer. Wheaton: Crossway, 1994.

Lincoln, Andrew T. *Ephesians*. Vol. 42 of Word Biblical Commentary. Dallas: Word, 1990.

Lloyd, John Wills, Edward J. Kameenui, and David Chard, eds. *Issues in Educating Students with Disabilities*. Mahwah, N.J.: Routledge, 1997.

Longman III, Tremper. *Proverbs*. Baker Commentary on the Old Testament Wisdom and Psalms. Grand Rapids: Baker, 2006.

Low, Keith. "ADHD and Diet: Improving ADHD Symptoms with Diet." Available from http://add.about.com/od/childrenandteens/a/Nutrition.htm. Internet; accessed 14 August 2012.

MacArthur, John F., Jr. *2 Timothy*. MacArthur New Testament Commentary. Chicago: Moody Press, 1995.

————. *Ephesians*. MacArthur New Testament Commentary. Chicago: Moody, 1986.

————. "Parenting in an Anti-Spanking Culture." Available from http://www.gty.org/Resources/articles/3127. Internet; accessed 7 December 2012.

————. *Philippians*. MacArthur New Testament Commentary. Chicago: Moody, 2001.

————. *What the Bible Says about Parenting: God's Plan for Rearing Your Child*. Nashville: Word, 2000.

McCabe, Robert V. *Old Testament Studies: Interpreting Proverbs*. Available from http://www.oldtestamentstudies.org/my-papers/other-papers/wisdom-literature/interpreting-proverbs. Internet; accessed 20 April, 2013.

McKane, William. *Proverbs: A New Approach*. Philadelphia: Westminster, 1970.

Meek, Will. "TV & ADHD." Available from http://psychcentral.com/blog/ archives/ 2007/09/08/tv-adhd/. Internet; accessed 16 September 2010.

Menhard, Francha Roffé. *Drugs: The Facts about Ritalin*. New York: Marshall Cavendish Benchmark, 2007.

Moll, Carl Bernhard. *The Psalms*. Translated and edited by Charles Biggs, John Forsyth, James Hammond, and Fred McCurdy. Vol. 9 of *Lange's Commentary on the Holy Scriptures*. Edited by Philip Schaff. 1872; reprint, Grand Rapids: Zondervan, n.d.

Monastra, Vincent J. *Parenting Children with ADHD: 10 Lessons that Medicine Cannot Teach*. Washington, D.C.: American Psychological Association, 2005.

Moo, Douglas J. *James: An Introduction and Commentary*. Vol. 16 of Tyndale New Testament Commentaries. Downers Grove: InterVarsity, 1985.

Morganthaler, Timothy. "How Many Hours of Sleep Are Enough for Good Health?" Available from http://www.mayoclinic.org/healthy-living/adult-health/expert-answers/how-many-hours-of-sleep-are-enough/faq-20057898. Internet; accessed 21 May 2014.

Moss, Robert. *Why Johnny Can't Concentrate: Coping with Attention Deficit Problems*. New York: Bantam, 1990.

Motyer, J. Alec. *Isaiah: An Introduction and Commentary*. Vol. 20 of Tyndale Old Testament Commentaries. Edited by Donald J. Wiseman. Downers Grove: InterVarsity, 1999.

Mounce, William D. *Pastoral Epistles*. Edited by Ralph P. Martin and Lynn A. Losie. Vol. 46 of Word Biblical Commentary. New York: Thomas Nelson, 2000.

National Institute of Neurological Disorders and Strokes. "Brain Basics: Understanding Sleep." Available from http://www.ninds.nih.gov/disorders/brain_basics/ understanding_sleep.htm. Internet; accessed 14 August 2012.

Neven, Ruth S., Vicki Anderson, and Tim Godber. *Rethinking ADHD: An Illness of Our Time*. Sydney, Australia: Allen and Unwin, 2002.

Newheiser, Jim. *Opening Up Proverbs*. Leominster, England: Day One Publications, 2008.

Nigg, Joel. *What Causes ADHD? Understanding What Goes Wrong and Why*. New York: Guilford, 2006.

Norcross, John, ed. *Psychotherapy, Relationships That Work: Therapist Contributions and Responsiveness to Patients*. New York: Oxford University, 2002.

Nordqvist, Christian. "Premature Babies Much More Likely to Have ADHD." Available from http://www.medicalnewstoday.com/articles/44574.php. Internet; accessed 18 September 2010.

O'Dell, Nancy, and Patricia Cook. *Stopping ADHD: A Unique and Proven Drug-Free Program for Treating ADHD Children and Adults*. New York: Avery, 2004.

Ohene, S. A., M. Ireland, C. McNeely, and I.W. Borowsky. "Parental Expectations, Physical Punishment, and Violence among Adolescents Who Score Positive on a Psychosocial Screening Test in Primary Care." *Pediatrics* 117, no. 6 (2006): 441-47.

Olasky, Marvin. "Psychology Today: What Should Christians Make of Neuroscience?" *World Magazine*, September 8, 2012.

Owen, Jim. *Christian Psychology's War on God's Word: The Victimization of the Believer*. Stanley, N.C.: Timeless Texts, 1993.

Oz, Cengiz. "Could You Have ADHD?" Available from http://www.doctoroz.com/quiz/could-you-have-adhd. Internet; accessed 16 September 2010.

Pantley, Elizabeth. "Should Babies and Toddlers Watch Television?" Available from http://pregnancy.about.com/od/yourbaby/a/babiesandtv.htm. Internet; accessed 20 May 2008.

Parvaresh, Nooshin, Ziaaddini Hassan, Kheradmand Ali, and Bayati Hamidreza. "Attention Deficit Hyperactivity Disorder (ADHD) and Conduct Disorder in Children of Drug Dependent Parents." *Addiction and Health* 2, no. 3-4 (Summer and Autumn 2010): 89-94.

Pennington, Bruce. *Diagnosing Learning Disorders: A Neuropsychological Framework*. 2nd ed. New York: Guilford, 2009.

Petersen, Melody. *Our Daily Meds*. New York: Sarah Crichton Books, 2008.

Phillips, Dan. *God's Wisdom In Proverbs: Hearing God's Voice in Scripture*. The Woodlands, Tex.: Kress Biblical Resources, 2011.

Pliszka, Steven R. *Treating ADHD and Comorbid Disorders: Psychosocial and Psychopharmacological Interventions*. New York: Guilford, 2009.

Pressman, Robert, and Steve Imber. "Relationship of Children's Daytime

Behavior Problems with Bedtime Routines/Practices: A Family Context and the Consideration of Faux-ADHD." Available from http://www.pedipsyc.com/abstract_FauxADHD.php. Internet; accessed 21 September 2011.

Rice, David. "Psychotherapy for Oppositional-Defiant Kids with Low Frustration Tolerance." Available from http://www.psychotherapy.net/article/oppositional-defiants-kids. Internet; accessed 15 September 2010.

Rief, Sandra F. *How to Reach and Teach ADD/ADHD Children: Practical Techniques, Strategies, and Interventions for Helping Children with Attention Problems and Hyperactivity*. West Nyack, N.Y.: Center for Applied Research in Education, 1993.

Ritalin Death. "Conditions that Mimic ADD or ADHD." Available from http://www.ritalindeath.com/Conditions-that-Mimic-ADHD.htm. Internet; accessed 17 September 2010.

Rosemond, John, and Bose Ravenel. *The Diseasing of America's Children: Exposing the ADHD Fiasco and Empowering Parents to Take Back Control*. Dallas: Thomas Nelson, 2008.

Saul, Richard Saul. *ADHD Does Not Exist: The Truth about Attention Deficit and Hyperactivity Disorder*. New York: HarperCollins, 2014.

Scott, Stuart, and Heath Lambert, eds. *Counseling the Hard Cases: True Stories Illustrating the Sufficiency of God's Resources in Scripture*. Nashville: B&H, 2012.

Silver, Larry. *Dr. Larry Silver's Advice to Parents on Attention-Deficit Hyperactivity Disorder*. Washington, D.C.: American Psychiatric Press Inc., 1993.

Southall, Angela. *The Other Side of ADHD: Attention Deficit Hyperactivity Disorder Exposed and Explained*. Abingdon, England: Radcliffe, 2007.

Spence-Jones, H. D. M., ed. *Romans*. The Pulpit Commentary. New York: Funk and Wagnalls Company, 1909.

Spurgeon, Charles H. *An All-Round Ministry*. London: Banner of Truth, n.d.

———. *The Treasury of David*. Vol 2. New York: Funk and Wagnalls, 1885.

Stein, David. *Ritalin Is Not the Answer*. San Francisco: Jossey-Bass Publishers, 1999.

Stein, Martin T. "When Preschool Children Have ADHD." Available from http://pediatrics.jwatch.org/cgi/content/full/2007/110/1. Internet; accessed 17 September 2010.

Still, George. "Some Abnormal Physical Conditions in Children." *Lancet Medical Journal* 1 (1902): 1008-12.

Szasz, Thomas S. *Pharmacracy: Medicine and Politics in America*. New York: Praeger, 2001.

Tavris, Carol. *Psychobabble and Biobunk: Using Psychological Science to Think Critically about Popular Psychology.* Upper Saddle River, N.J.: Prentice Hall, 2001.

Taylor, John. *Helping Your ADD Child: Hundreds of Practical Solutions for Parents and Teachers of ADD Children and Teens - with or without Hyperactivity.* Roseville, Calif.: Prima Publishing, 2001.

Thompson, J. A. *Deuteronomy: An Introduction and Commentary.* Vol. 5 of Tyndale Old Testament Commentaries. Edited by Donald J. Wiseman. Downers Grove: InterVarsity, 1974.

Thorlakson, Catherine. "The Experience of Learning for Youth Diagnosed with Attention Deficit Hyperactivity Disorder." PhD diss., Capella University, 2010.

Thornton, Stephen P. "Sigmund Freud (1856-1939)." Available from http://www.iep.utm.edu/freud/#H2. Internet; accessed 21 April 2014

Tripp, Tedd. *Shepherding a Child's Heart.* Wapwallopen, Pa.: Shepherd Press, 1995.

Turner, Barry. "ADHD and the Meaning of Evidence." Available from http://www.ritalindeath.com/ADHD-Evidence.htm. Internet; accessed 17 September 2010.

Waltke, Bruce. *The Book of Proverbs: Chapters 1-15.* New International Commentary on the Old Testament. Edited by R. K. Harrison and Robert L. Hubbard Jr. Grand Rapids: Eerdmans, 2004.

————. *The Book of Proverbs: Chapters 15-30.* New International Commentary on the Old Testament. Edited by R. K. Harrison and Robert L. Hubbard Jr. Grand Rapids: Eerdmans, 2004.

————. "Does Proverbs Promise Too Much?" *Andrews University Seminary Studies* 34 (1996): 319-36.

WebMD. "ADHD and Sleep Disorders." Available from http://www.webmd.com/add-adhd/guide/adhd-sleep-disorders. Internet; accessed 14 August 2012.

————. "ADHD Diets." Available from http://www.webmd.com/add-adhd/guide/adhd-diets?page=2. Internet; accessed 14 August 2012.

————. "Stimulant Drugs for ADHD." Available from http://www.webmd.com/add-adhd/guide/adhd-stimulant-therapy. Internet; accessed 10 July 2011.

Weiss, Gabrielle, and Lily Trokenberg Hectman. *Hyperactive Children Grown Up: ADHD in Children, Adolescents, and Adults.* 2nd ed. New York: Guilford, 1993.

164

Weiss, Robin. "Babies and TV." Available from http://pregnancy.about.com/od/yourbaby/a/babiesandtv.htm. Internet; accessed 11 August 2010.

Welch, Edward. *A.D.D. Wandering Minds and Wired Bodies*. Phillipsburg, N.J.: Presbyterian and Reformed, 1999.

———. *Blame it on the Brain? Distinguishing Chemical Imbalances, Brain Disorders, and Disobedience*. Phillipsburg, N.J.: Presbyterian and Reformed, 1998.

Wender, Paul. *ADHD: Attention-Deficit Hyperactivity Disorder in Children, Adolescents, and Adults*. New York: Oxford University Press, 2000.

———. *The Hyperactive Child, Adolescent, and Adult: Attention Deficit Disorder through the Lifespan*. New York: Oxford University Press, 1987.

Wiersbe, Warren W. *Be Skillful: Tapping God's Guidebook to Fulfillment*. Wheaton: Victor Books, 1996.

Whybray, R. N. *Proverbs*. New Century Bible Commentary. Grand Rapids: Eerdmans, 1994.

Yager, Joel. "New Findings in the Pathogenesis, Genetics, and Comorbidity of ADHD." *Journal Watch Psychiatry*, December 30, 2005. Available from http://pediatrics.jwatch.org/cgi/content/full/2005/1230/9. Internet; accessed 17 September 2010.